LES HIGGINS
FOREWORD BY MITCHELL E. CORDER

LEADERSHIP THOUGHTS

CHALLENGING LOCAL CHURCH
LEADERS TO MOVE FORWARD

© 2024 Les Higgins
LEADERSHIP THOUGHTS

All rights reserved. No part of this publication may be reproduced, stored in a retrieval system, or transmitted in any form or by any means, electronic, mechanical, photocopying, recording, or otherwise without the prior permission of the publisher or in accordance with the provisions of the Copyright, Designs and Patents Act 1988 or under the terms of any license permitting limited copying issued by the Copyright Licensing Agency.

Unless otherwise noted, all scriptures are from the New King James Version®. Copyright© 1982 by Thomas Nelson, Inc. Used by permission. All rights reserved.

Scripture quotations marked NLT are taken from the Holy Bible, New Living Translation, Copyright © 1996, 2004, 2015 by Tyndale House Foundation. Used by permission of Tyndale House Publishers, Inc., Carol Stream, Illinois 60188. All rights reserved.

Scripture quotations marked (MEV) are taken from The Holy Bible, Modern English Version. Copyright© 2014 by Military Bible Association. Published and distributed by Charisma House.

Library of Congress Control Number: 2024913919

ISBN: 979-8-218-45130-1

Published by:
Resurgence Publishing, LLC
P.O. Box 514
Goshen, OH 45122
www.resurgencebooks.org

Cover Design: Aaftab Sheikh

Printed in the United States of America

Dedication

The book is dedicated to a special group of servant leaders who are not only important, they are essential!

Local Church Pastors

The ministry of the local church moves forward because of the involvement of many—it does, indeed, take a team. But as is the case with any team, there must be that voice at the helm giving clear direction and helping everyone head in the right direction. This is the job of the pastor—hear from God, deliver that message and lead people in the way of the Lord.

Pastors rarely receive the accolades they deserve. Some are compensated well while most depend on a salary from secular employment to make it possible for them to lead a local congregation. Some serve in prominent places while most labor in obscurity. Some are recognized for their accomplishments while most await their reward in eternity. Through it all, these chosen individuals lead and love. They are truly gifts from God.

This book is written for them and the leaders who serve with them. May their lives be enriched by its pages.

"Therefore, my beloved brethren, be steadfast, immovable, always abounding in the work of the Lord, knowing that your labor is not in vain in the Lord." I Corinthians 15:58

Table of Contents

Foreword 6

Preface 9

1. Follow The Instructions 12
2. Stop, Look And Listen 18
3. Essential In The Kingdom 26
4. You Are Stronger Than You Think 32
5. Some Things Are Just Sacred 38
6. The Promise Is For You 46
7. Keep Your Eye On The Ball 52
8. More Than A Message 58
9. Revival...Will We Know It When We See It? 64
10. The Spotlight Keeps Coming Back To Me 70
11. I Am Human But I Am His! 78
12. Awakening Is On The Way 84
13. Your Church—A Lake Or A River? 92

14. Keeping The Faith On Saturday	100
15. A Safe Place To Turn Around	108
16. It's Harvest Time!	116
17. What We've Got Here Is Failure To Communicate	124
18. God Is Speaking—Are You Listening?	132
19. It's Going To Take Some Time	140
20. The Call To Swim Upstream	146
21. Making Healing Front And Center	154
22. The Blessing Of Barrenness	162
23. Rising To The Challenge	170
24. When God Is Silent	176
25. God Is Calling—Will You Answer?	182
26. This World Needs Us!	188
27. But The Church Prayed	196
28. Even When Your Faith Is Not Strong	202
29. Sometimes Praying Is Not Enough	208
30. He Sees, He Knows And Payday Is Coming	216
31. Do Not—And I Repeat—Do Not Drink The Poison	222
32. Some Things For You To Think About	230

Foreword

John Maxwell, a well-known leadership expert, says, "Leadership is influence—nothing more, nothing less." Leadership is influence, but communication is how leaders influence others. Communicators have great content and know how to connect with people. Bishop Les Higgins is a gifted communicator.

This book is filled with great content—information that will interest, instruct, and inspire those who read it. Reading it is like talking to a wise friend!

The thoughts found in this book are really words of wisdom that are the result of knowledge and experience gained from a leader who has spent over 40 years serving the local church. The insights, principles, and truth found in it comes from someone who loves the church and believes in those who serve it.

This book is written for those in ministry leadership but focuses on the leaders themselves. Specifically, it is written for Christian leaders—men and women who have been called to serve the Lord through His Church locally and globally.

Ministry leadership results in influence but begins with a calling. Leaders are called to lead. Our confidence as leaders begins with our acknowledgment God has chosen us for the role that we serve. Our growth continues as we continue to develop in our calling to lead. Growing ministers lead growing ministries.

Each chapter of the book is a leadership lesson, a self-contained teaching that is designed to increase leadership competency so you will be more fully equipped to fulfill God's call for your life. What makes these lessons so beneficial is that they are (1) Biblical: based on spiritual principles; (2) Practical: you can put them into practice; and (3) Applicable: they apply to any context of ministry leadership.

Ministry leadership is different from any other type of leadership. The local church is different in its function and purpose than any other type of organization. It does not exist for itself; it exists for the benefit of others and for a purpose that has eternal consequences.

Ministry leaders deal with problems and challenges that are unique to the church—challenges other organizations do not face. One of the challenges of leading in a local church is that we are tasked with accomplishing supernatural ministry in a natural world. Understanding that tension and knowing how to balance, both the practical and spiritual aspects of ministry, can be a daunting task. This book can help!

Growth as a ministry leader is more about progress than it is promotion, more about moving forward than moving up. Whether you are a seasoned leader or someone who is just starting on your leadership journey—a first-chair or second-chair leader—this book will challenge you and build your confidence as a leader.

The key to growth as a leader is knowing how to apply what you have learned. In order to facilitate the learning process, there are questions for discussion at the conclusion of each chapter. They are designed to help you maximize the benefits of the material in this book.

Here's what I know, as you read and apply the leadership thoughts shared in this book, you will be a better, bolder leader with competence and confidence. Get ready to grow.

Bishop Higgins has made a significant contribution through this book for the development of those who have been called to serve and lead in the local church. I highly recommend it both for personal study and as a resource for staff and leadership development.

"For we are His workmanship, created in Christ Jesus for good works, which God prepared beforehand that we should walk in them." Ephesians 2:10

Mitchell E. Corder, Director
Church Health and Evangelism
Church of God—Cleveland, Tennessee

Preface

It is still hard to believe it happened. Had I not experienced it myself I would probably say it was fake news. In 2020, a pandemic shutdown the world! For the only time in my lifetime it seemed like everything came to a halt, we were not sure how to respond, and no one knew what was coming next. It was a traumatic time, indeed.

Many years ago, as a young college student at the University of Oklahoma, I accepted the call of God to preach His Word. That calling became my life as I took my responsibility seriously and traveled from coast to coast spreading the Gospel. I was given opportunities to serve in many ministerial roles, but I always knew my first call was to preach. But that pandemic...that awful pandemic...cleared my calendar and forced me into silence. This was a place I—and you—had never been.

While sitting in my home study one morning, thinking about the many creative ways local churches were continuing to perform ministry during the shutdown, it dawned on me there was nothing preventing me from delivering a message via social media. I would not be standing before a congregation, as was my tradition, but I could still share a word in written form. I may even be able to reach people who would never hear me preach a sermon. This could actually be a tool God uses to bless somebody. Thus, my blog was born.

I must admit I was a little surprised at the far-reaching affect the blog would have. As I began receiving my monthly readership report, I discovered people from all over the country and other nations of the world were reading my words. Sitting at my computer and writing on average between 1200—1500 words, I was conveying thoughts that had the potential of making a difference. Even a pesky virus could not stop that!

Today, I am back to accepting appointments and preaching sermons that I believe the Lord has placed on my heart. It feels even better than before to walk into a sanctuary for worship and the Word with real live people. But the lesson I learned during the pandemic about the power of the written word has not escaped me. I am going to keep writing, believing the message will go where I never will.

The book you hold in your hand is a compilation of some of the blogs I have posted online. Each contains a message intended to challenge, encourage and instruct readers from all walks of life, but especially local church leaders. I really believe these special individuals called by God to direct ministry in local churches of all styles and sizes will benefit from these thoughts. These articles were written with these leaders in mind.

LEADERSHIP THOUGHTS—Challenging Local Church Leaders to Move Forward is intended to provoke the reader to good works. The benefit of it will not come from simply reading it but acting upon it. To assist in this process, there are thought producing questions at the end of each chapter along with a prayer assignment. I believe when you seriously consider these questions, with your ministry context in mind, and follow through with a time of prayer, your effectiveness as a leader will be impacted greatly. Something good is going to happen in you and through you!

God is using the local church. If there was ever a doubt of its importance to God and His Kingdom, the pandemic erased all of those doubts. What had the potential to destroy us made us stronger. When we could not meet in our buildings, methods were created to continue ministry. More people heard the Gospel during this season than at any other time in history. Hell and all of its forces could not stop what the Holy Spirit started. The Church is alive and continues to be a mighty force for good in this world.

God really does have a plan for your church, and you are a big part of that plan. His mighty hand is upon you and His will is to work through you to accomplish great things for the cause of Christ. You cannot become stale and stagnant. You cannot become weary in well doing. You cannot become satisfied with your present position. The call to local church leaders is to get up and move forward. We need you to be healthy and strong. We need you to be passionate and faithful. We need you to be everything God has called you to be.

You have a tool, here, to help. Read it. Pray it through. Act upon it. I have a feeling you are never going to be the same! Let's do this!

CHAPTER 1
Follow The Instructions
(POSTED MARCH 21, 2020)

FOLLOW THE INSTRUCTIONS

As I write this article, the rain is pouring down outside my window. I can see and hear it, but I am perfectly dry and safe inside my residence. The elements outside are not pleasant right now but I am safely sheltered from the storm in my nice, warm home.

This reminds me of another storm that raged many years ago for the Children of Israel. For 400 years they were slaves in Egypt. The last many years of their enslavement was marked by cruel treatment administered by Pharaoh the king. The Israelites cried for mercy but it seemed there would be none. But in fact, God had heard their prayers and a plan for their exodus was in place.

Moses, the leader of the people, was directed by God to appear before Pharaoh and demand the Israelites be set free. The king's heart was hardened and, in spite of great plagues sent by God upon the land, he refused to let the people go. But the most severe of all plagues is about to be unleashed—the death of the firstborn in every family.

God instructed Moses to call for preparation, on the part of the Children of Israel, for this last plague. They would be exempted from the impending devastation only if they carefully followed the instructions. A great storm is about to ravage Egypt but a means of escape will be provided for the people of God.

The instructions called for a lamb to be killed and its blood applied to the door posts and over each door of every home of the Children of Israel. As the death angel moves across the country on this stormy night, he will pass over every residence where the blood is applied. They were also instructed to cook and eat the lamb; they were to be fully dressed with their staff in hand and they were to request valuable gifts from the Egyptians.

These instructions seemed strange to the people, I'm sure, but they followed them completely. The night of the last plague comes and a great cry arises from all over Egypt. Death prevailed throughout the country but all was well in Goshen where the Children of Israel lived. Pharaoh has had enough—he orders the people of God to quickly leave his country. Freedom and victory come to the Israelites!

Our world is presently in the midst of a great storm. Most of us have never lived through anything remotely resembling this pandemic. There is much panic and fear throughout our country and across the globe. No one knows when this thing will end and what the world will look like when it is over. But deep in my spirit I hear the voice of God saying, "I've got a plan. Just follow my instructions."

All my life I've been hearing about a great revival coming to America. We've seen times of stirring we thought might lead to this awakening, but our hearts long to see more. Could it be that this crisis is an event that will propel the Church to the promised outpouring of the Spirit, and could it be the events happening all around the world will lead masses of people to call on the Lord? I honestly hope and fervently pray the answer to these questions is yes! But there's a catch...we must follow the instructions.

THE BLOOD MUST BE APPLIED

God is not looking for slick professionals who know more than anyone else; He's looking for the blood. He is not looking for programs and methods guaranteed to bring astounding results; He's looking for the blood. He's not looking for large bank accounts, plush sanctuaries or the latest, greatest anything; He is looking for people who have no greater claim than they once were lost but now they're found, and the blood of Jesus covers their sins. We are saved by the blood, kept by the blood and made overcomers by the blood of the Lamb!

JESUS MUST BE AT THE CENTER OF ALL WE DO

The Children of Israel were told the lamb must be completely eaten; nothing was to be wasted. I believe He is saying to us today, "Jesus must receive our full attention and allegiance. Nothing and no one can be more important." That night in Egypt, nothing mattered more than the lamb. The same must be true today.

Unfortunately, we find ourselves in a time of much ego-centered and personality-driven ministry. Men have become the face of ministry and many in the church identify more with that man than they do with our Lord. It must be clearly understood, however, revival will come through Jesus, not through celebrated men. Now is the time to declare, "I must decrease that He might increase."

WE MUST BE FULLY DRESSED AND READY TO MOVE QUICKLY

Some will miss this coming revival because they have not made preparation. Some are asleep while others are living in the past. Some are listening to the wrong voices and have become encumbered with devices that attach them more to the world than the Spirit. Some are leaning on the arm of the flesh, convinced their way is the right way. All of this must stop right now!

We will only be prepared when we immerse ourselves in the Word, worship and prayer. When our hearts are fully tuned to the Holy Spirit, we will receive our marching orders and ministry assignments. We will be anointed and empowered beyond our wildest imagination. The weak will become strong. The church will become THE CHURCH. Revival will sweep across the land.

WE SHOULD EXPECT GREAT INCREASE

This revival will not be for our gratification; it is coming for His Kingdom to be increased. As the Gospel goes forth and Jesus is lifted up, He will be drawing men, women, boys and girls to Him. The harvest is coming! (And I say this by the Spirit, "get ready; the harvest is coming!")

I truly believe, at the same time as this ingathering of souls, God is going to bless His people and make them a testimony to the world. Those who delight themselves in Him will receive the desires of their heart. It is the Father's pleasure to give the Kingdom to His children. His children will have everything they need to do what He has called them to do.

I'm watching the storm clouds roll over us and, I must admit, at times I feel afraid. But it is in these moments of fear I am gently reminded I am safe in the arms of Jesus. He is with me and He has a plan. His plan will not bring harm to me but it places me right in the middle of what He wants to do in this world in these last days. He has brought me to the Kingdom for this time. He has purposely chosen me to participate in a great revealing of His power and glory. I'm honored to be His son and servant. I'm determined to stick close, listen carefully and follow His instructions.

AN EXERCISE IN CONTEMPLATION
Placing What I Just Read Into My Ministry Context

1. What are your takeaways from this chapter? How can it be applied to your life and ministry?

2. When you pray about your ministry, what do you hear God saying to you? Have you fully surrendered to His instructions? If not, why not?

3. Describe what you envision when you think about God having His full way in your church/ministry. What role do you play, personally, in ensuring God's will is fully done in your church/ministry?

PRAYER ASSIGNMENT

Spend quality time praying for God to give unobstructed vision for your church/ministry. Be willing to sacrifice your own agenda and plans as you submit to His. Ask God for a strategy to accomplish His will for you. Listen intently for the voice of the Holy Spirit as He begins to unfold His plan. Determine to obey.

CHAPTER 2

Stop, Look And Listen

(Posted April 4, 2020)

Many years ago, as a result of a much-publicized safety campaign, a slogan was created to place at railroad crossings to alert oncoming traffic of an approaching railroad track. The slogan was simple and to the point, but the message was crystal clear. Drivers were told to Stop, Look and Listen. No doubt many lives were saved because of this posted message.

As I write this article, the world is experiencing a massive pandemic unlike anything we have seen in our lifetime. Each day numbers rise of those infected by Covid-19 and no one seems to know when it will end. Scientific researchers are working feverishly to find a cure and our dedicated medical professionals are working around-the-clock to save as many lives as possible. I, like so many others, am praying for divine intervention. We know God is able to move and give us an "only God could have done it" ending to this crisis.

But as I pray, I keep sensing there is something God is wanting to do before it all goes away. (I'm not saying God has caused this crisis, but He is certainly working through it.) I'm sure I don't know the full extent of it, but I believe He is working through this trial of fire with the intent of bringing us out as pure gold. He is speaking and revelation is coming to those who are listening. The foundation of every realm of our society is being shaken, but I am confident the result will be the discovery of things that cannot be shaken. This is a challenging time, no doubt, but it could be a pivotal point in history if we will allow the plan of God to have its full effect.

As I sit in my home during this time of quarantine, my mind is being drawn back to a childhood memory of that railroad crossing sign. Those three words of warning are being illuminated in my spirit and I sense God is speaking to me. It

LEADERSHIP THOUGHTS

just could be, that simple sign from a long time ago could be direction for our present situation.

STOP!

A few weeks ago, our world totally changed. It's like we went to bed one night and woke up the next morning in a totally different time. The way we were used to doing business couldn't be done anymore. We've been forced to find new ways to do just about everything—work, education, church... It's unbelievable!

I am especially encouraged, however, by the way the church has rallied to ensure the work and message of Jesus Christ continues to be communicated. As a matter of fact, more people are hearing the message today than at any other time in history! The church has, indeed, left the building and is being deployed across the globe.

But here is my concern—we must not use this time to simply find new ways to do what we have always done. The familiar may need to be our short-term response but we cannot settle there. This is the season to expand our borders and go where we've dreamed about going, but could never quite reach. This will not happen while we are speeding down the much-traveled highway of the expected. It will only come to those who are willing to slow down and take some time to get into His presence.

If we will stop long enough, we will discover the Holy Spirit is doing a fresh, new thing in His Church. The new wine of the Spirit is being made available to those desiring it. We must not let the "busyness" of continuation keep us from receiving this blessing.

LOOK!

Several years ago, I drove a van full of fellow ministers to a conference. One of my friends, who was an avid outdoorsman, sat in the middle seat directly behind me and leaned forward to talk throughout the entire trip. Our discussions were non-stop about a variety of subjects. As we would be waxing warm on some topic, my friend would quickly insert, "Look, there is a hawk on that high-line wire!" I would look and, sure enough, I would see that beautiful bird. We would continue our conversation when suddenly my friend would say, "Look, there is a deer out in that field." I would look and, sure enough, I would see the deer. This kind of interruption happened many times as we traveled and talked that day.

As much time as I spent driving every week, I rarely saw God's beautiful creation the way I did that day traveling with my friend. He seemed to have a sixth sense when it came to spotting wildlife. Then it hit me—my friend loved and spent a lot of time in the outdoors. He had trained his eyes to see what I usually missed. Regardless of what was going on, part of him was tuned in to spot what he truly enjoyed. Then the life-lesson came—you usually see what you are looking for!

I have tried to apply this lesson throughout my life as I've approached various situations. I believe it is especially applicable to where we find ourselves in the church right now. We need spiritual eyes that are open to see what the Holy Spirit is wanting to show us.

Somehow we must learn to look past the clutter that is dominating our attention. We've got to see the ripened harvest we have not yet touched. We've got to see the laborers God has called, but we have not yet noticed. We have got to see the opportunities that heretofore we have not even considered. We have got to see what the carnal mind misses and only the spiritually attuned and sensitive eyes can behold.

LEADERSHIP THOUGHTS

LISTEN!

A lot of different voices are speaking today. The media, politicians and experts from all walks of life are giving us their opinion and influencing our thinking. The noise is deafening and, quite frankly, alarming. Whereas we should not be ignorant of issues of the day, and we need good information to make sound decisions, I'm afraid much of what we are hearing is more fear-driven than it is faith-driven. Not all voices deserve our attention.

In the process of sifting through the many voices in my ear right now, I seem to be hearing a still, small voice asking a question that deserves an answer, "What is the Spirit saying to the church?" I have no doubt He is speaking and what He is saying needs to be heard. I don't want to assume I know what it is. My assumption is probably clouded by my heritage and experience. I don't want to miss this divine revelation because I think I already know. I owe it to myself, and those I serve, to listen to the One who is all-knowing and has a plan already devised for my victory.

In the mid '80s, I lived in a city with a General Motors Assembly plant. It was announced one day, a decision had been made to discontinue production of the vehicle being built at that particular location. A new vehicle model would begin production in a few months, but in the meantime the plant would be closed. It was being closed for retooling. The tools and processes needed to build the old car would not work for the new one. It would take a little while to make the necessary changes, but once they were made, the plant would reopen to maximum capacity and a new, exciting model of vehicle would begin production.

Could it be...could it be, this is what the church is experiencing right now? Could it be, the message that has been preached all my life about a last day revival and a massive ingathering of the harvest is about to happen? Could it be, the tools and processes that have brought us to this place will not be the same ones needed in this new season? Could it be, God is giving us an opportunity to evaluate and fix, evaluate and shore-up or evaluate and change? Could it be, this is our time to reset? Could it be...could it be?

I think I can say with a true sense of certainty, when this pandemic ends (and it will) our world will look a lot different than it did before this whole thing started. This prediction is not intended to be gloomy and negative. As a matter of fact, I've never been more excited about my future and ministry than I am right now! I have lived for this moment—I get to be part of a great spiritual outpouring! I don't want to miss it. I have chosen to use this time to prepare my heart and allow God to work in me. My heart cries out, "Here am I, Lord. Send me."

I challenge you to get ready for something truly spectacular in your life and ministry! Refuse to let fear have a place in your heart. Remember to whom you belong and know He has called you to the Kingdom for such a time as this. Don't get comfortable though...don't settle. God wants to do something fresh in you. He wants to take you where you've never been. It's time for those God-dreams to come true. It is your time! This will all become clear if you are willing to Stop, Look and Listen.

AN EXERCISE IN CONTEMPLATION
Placing What I Just Read Into My Ministry Context

1. What are your takeaways from this chapter? How can it be applied to your life and ministry?

2. How difficult is it for you to "turn off" the chatter around you and "turn on" the voice of the Holy Spirit? What do you need to do for this to happen in your life? Are you willing to intentionally stop, look and listen for the Holy Spirit in your life and ministry?

3. Are there some changes that need to be made in your life/ministry in order for you to reap your harvest and be all you can be for God in this season? What are some of the needed changes you see? What is keeping you from making these changes?

PRAYER ASSIGNMENT

Find a quiet place to be alone with God. Be intentional, even if only for a few minutes, to lay aside the busyness of your life in order to experience His peaceful presence. Allow Him to speak to you and sharpen your vision to see what He wants you to see. Be willing for Him to place you on the potter's wheel in order to remake and remold you into His perfect plan. Be sure to thank Him for the work He is doing in you. Make this prayer a regular part of your life.

CHAPTER 3
Essential In The Kingdom
(Posted April 14, 2020)

The dictionary defines the word essential as absolutely necessary; extremely important. During this current pandemic, the government has found it necessary to decide which businesses it deems essential and which ones are not. Businesses have had to make the same call with their employees. Many of these decisions have been met with controversy and caused great pain. We have discovered it is very hard to come to a consensus in such an important matter.

Recently, during a time of prayer and meditation, I began to think about Kingdom essentials. I thought about today's church and wondered how God saw it. I thought about many things that happen every day under the cover of religion and asked myself, "Does God view these things to be important?" I thought about many of our church traditions (ministries) and began to consider if they still serve a useful purpose and would the Father call them vital to His plan.

Quite frankly, this exercise was somewhat uncomfortable. I have spent my life serving God through His church. Because of my deep love for the church, I sometimes become very defensive and find it hard to be critical. But on this particular day, I felt the need to look deep and let the Lord speak to me.

Over the years it has been easy for many churches to be judgmental toward the world and even other churches, but the inward look was one they chose not to take. They have continued to stir in the ashes of a long-passed revival and found solace in what God did there in a bygone day. As attendance decreases and community impact becomes almost non-existent, they continue to claim the promise, "The gates of hell will not prevail against the church." Something isn't right.

It seems to me, the time has come for the spotlight to turn toward us. What does God see when He looks at us? What should our focus be? What ensures we make the essential list? It's really not that complicated but it is important. Maybe we could start by answering the following questions:

IS JESUS BEING LIFTED UP?

The church has always been prone to identify with personalities. Even in the New Testament, we read of groups in the church at Corinth who attached themselves to Apollos while others identified with Paul. The same occurs today. Some follow a preacher while others link themselves to a church/denomination. Whereas there is no problem having a favorite preacher or committing to a church, our first allegiance must be to Jesus. Intentional effort must be made by church leaders to ensure people are being pointed to Jesus. Any effort to elevate man or ministry over Jesus is nothing short of idolatry.

IS FRUIT BEING PRODUCED?

It is the Father's plan for His church to bear fruit. *"Every branch in Me that does not bear fruit He takes away; and every branch that bears fruit He prunes, that it may bear more fruit."* (John 15:2 NKJV) Stagnant, stale, cold, lifeless...these can never be words associated with His church. Something must be happening—life must be happening! People must be growing and engaged in ministry. God is not concerned, as we are, with size or prominence; He is looking for fruit—fruit that remains to His glory.

IS GOD BLESSING?

Here is a simple rule of thumb for ministry—God blesses what He ordains. This does not mean there will not be trials and difficult seasons but, even in those times, you will see His hand and know He is with you. It's not your church; it's His. It's not your ministry; it's His. He will ensure His work accomplishes what it is intended to do.

The challenge is for us to make sure we are involved in ministry that He has, indeed, ordered. Instead of praying for God to bless your plan, ask God what plan He wants to bless. When we come to Him with a blank sheet of paper and allow Him to lead in our planning, He will take us to places of genuine victory and blessing. He will bless what He ordains.

WOULD ANYONE NOTICE IF YOU WENT AWAY?

This is such an ugly thought but one that should be considered. Ministry must be more than programs and profit; it must be about people. Kingdom efforts are vertically connected to God but horizontally connected to people.

Too often churches operate in a spiritually theoretical world and struggle with the practical. We know our goal is to save souls and prepare people for eternity, not fully realizing the way to accomplish this must pass through a person's reality. We want to get the Gospel into the hearts of people—we know that is their greatest need. But this will have a hard time happening if we don't understand that in order to get into someone's heart, we must first get into their world. It is this willingness to go where the people are that draws one to a ministry and to our Lord.

Over the past several months, the word shift has been used a lot by church leaders when discussing future ministry. What I think I understood, when I heard this word, was that change was coming—that there would be different and new ways of doing ministry. But I am really thinking now that it is much more than this. Deep in my heart, I believe the time has come for the essential to step up and the non-essential to step aside. We have arrived at a crucial moment in time.

LEADERSHIP THOUGHTS

These are days when the heavens and the earth are being shaken. We may not want to think about it, but church and how we do ministry is being affected by this shaking. Because of this, I reluctantly write, I believe the coming days will see a significant number of local churches/ministries close. This saddens me greatly, but some simply will not survive the challenges of these times.

But it is with great excitement I write, these times will see the greatest expansion of the Kingdom in the history of the world! The Holy Spirit is being poured out on those ministries who are opening themselves to Him. Those who are willing to dig deep into the wells of His Word will draw the water of His Spirit that will produce life in abundance! This is the day of miraculous multiplication! I really believe this!

The difference between those who do not survive and those who flourish is focusing on the elements God considers essential. Remember, God is not interested in protecting your posterity or promoting your personality, He is building His Kingdom! When we choose to fully partner with Him in this process, we overcome any and every obstacle in the way. We cannot lose!

I want you and me to make the cut. I want our churches and ministries to be essential to our Father. My prayer is, you will join me in doing whatever we have to do to ensure this happens.

AN EXERCISE IN CONTEMPLATION
Placing What I Just Read Into My Ministry Context

1. What are your takeaways from this chapter? How can it be applied to your life and ministry?

2. Answer the four questions mentioned in the chapter you just read. In your ministry, is Jesus being lifted up? Is fruit being produced? Is God blessing? Would anyone notice if you went away?

3. Is it possible there is a shift taking place in your ministry from areas that are no longer effective, or not as effective as they once were, to areas of ministry that will be more productive? Are you willing to make this shift? What needs to happen for this shift to occur?

PRAYER ASSIGNMENT

Ask God to shine His spotlight into your heart and reveal to you anything He wants to remove or change. Ask Him to help you determine the non-essentials that are taking your time and energy, and give you the courage to replace them with the things He deems essential. Recommit yourself to following Him with all of your heart. Take time to praise Him for the freshness He is bringing to your life and ministry.

CHAPTER 4

You Are Stronger Than You Think

(Posted April 23, 2020)

As the Covid-19 crisis was just getting started and before the stay-at-home orders were issued, I found myself one afternoon in a half-empty department store. It was actually a somewhat eerie experience. The shelves were already being emptied of many essential items. People were moving through the store quickly to secure what they needed. There was no conversation. Everyone seemed to be extremely focused and anxious to get their items and move on.

On this afternoon, even in the silence, I could sense the concern in my fellow shoppers. Panic was being communicated without words. It was easy to tell we were in a place we had never been and that was not a place in which anyone wanted to be. I must admit, in that moment, genuine fear moved into my spirit.

I immediately recognized what was happening to me and began to come against this fear. I began to declare the Word of the Lord and pray for God's protection and peace. This is an exercise I have repeated a few times since that day and, each time, I have felt the presence of the Holy Spirit move in close to remind me He had my family and me in the hollow of His hand. This reassurance has been just what the doctor ordered to sustain me in this season.

Times like these remind us how blessed we are to know Jesus and have Him living in our hearts. We go through the storms and experience their wrath, but something we cannot fully explain quiets us and gives unexplainable peace. I believe this something is the joy of the Lord.

Unfortunately, many believers seem to be succumbing to their storms. They have not forsaken the Lord, but their lives are far from what the Word declares they can be. Anxiety and fear are facts for them. Hope is distant and faith is constantly under attack. I don't mean to oversimplify this complicated situation but, if this describes you, I need to ask this question, "Have you checked your joy level?" It just might be, the answer to this real problem is a fresh encounter with the joy of the Lord.

King David, who was described as a man after God's own heart, sinned against God. When Nathan the prophet confronted him about his sin, David was broken and genuinely repented. Although he repented, David continued to struggle with the guilt of his action. This whole situation led him to pray a beautiful prayer, recorded in Psalm 51. In part of that prayer he cried out to God, *"Restore to me the joy of your salvation..." (Psalm 51:12 NKJV)*. It seems David was aware that a missing element in his life, at that moment, was the joy of the Lord. He knew this was something that had to be reestablished.

This divine gift is available to every believer. It is the Father's desire that this joy exist in abundance in everyone of His children. It cannot be attained in the world or from any of the world's pleasures, but it can always be found by taking the following three simple steps:

LOOK FOR GOD

This one is easy! God can always be found in the same place—the praise of His people. (Psalm 22:3) If you want to find God, begin to praise Him. Praise Him when you are hurting. Praise Him when you are lonely. Praise Him when you are tempted. Praise Him in the valley. Praise Him on the mountain. Praise Him when you feel like it and praise Him when you don't. Even when it requires great sacrifice on your part, give God your praise and discover His presence right then and there. There is not just a chance this will happen—it is a guarantee! God lives in your praise!

LIVE IN HIS PRESENCE

When I praise the Lord, even in my hard times, I become keenly aware of His presence. He moves in close to me and envelopes me in His love. The effect of this experience cannot be articulated or understood by human reasoning, but is extremely powerful to those who encounter it.

The key for me is to learn to practice His presence. What I mean is, I need to reach the place where coming into His presence is not an occasional action, but a true component of my existence. This happens when I make praise an element of my daily life.

There are so many benefits to this "praise/presence" lifestyle but one of the biggest is found in Psalm 16:11, *"...In Your presence is fullness of joy..."* When I get into the presence of God, I find joy! And do you notice the Psalmist does not say we receive a touch of joy, or that there is circumstantial joy? He says we find fullness of joy! A whole bunch of joy—more than you will ever need—will always be given to those who learn to live in the presence of the Lord!

LET THE GIFT WORK IN YOU

God's gifts are never simply feel-good experiences. He always has a purpose for what He does. This is certainly the case with joy. His purpose is found in Nehemiah 8:10, *"...The joy of the Lord is your strength."* You are made strong when His joy is working in your life.

You do not have to be weak. You do not have to be defeated by the bumps and bruises life sends your way. You may or may not be able to control the circumstances you face, but you have been equipped to be an overcomer. You are a winner. God knows it. The devil even knows it. The only one who needs convincing is you. You can have strength in your toughest battle. It will always, in every situation, be found in the joy of the Lord.

It does not take a rocket scientist to see our world is in turmoil. These chaotic times are bringing stress and anxiety to people everywhere. The only remedy I know is found in our Lord and in the joy He provides. Somehow, I believe He desires to showcase this joy in these troubled times by its reflection in your life. As those around you watch as you walk through your storm—and even through tears and pain—you exhibit joy that only comes from Him, He gets great glory, and you find unspeakable victory. This is the witness that cannot be duplicated in the world and the testimony that brings sinners to repentance.

There is great strength for you today. You will find it in the joy of the Lord. Praise Him. Live everyday in His presence. Let His plan for joy in your life be manifested. Pandemics or any other tool in the enemy's tool belt will not be a match for you. You are more than a conqueror. You were made for these times. You and Jesus have got this!

AN EXERCISE IN CONTEMPLATION
Placing What I Just Read Into My Ministry Context

1. What are your takeaways from this chapter? How can it be applied to your life and ministry?

2. Give some thought to an intense storm you have faced sometime in your life. Was God's presence with you in this storm? At what point did you fully recognize His presence? How did knowing He was with you affect your ability to overcome? What lessons did you learn from this storm?

3. Have you been able to draw from your experiences to help others? What are some ways God is using your experiences to bless others?

PRAYER ASSIGNMENT

Begin your prayer by thanking God for the many times He has brought you through your storms. Make yourself available for Him to use you to touch others who are experiencing storms in their lives. Ask Him to lead you to individuals that He wants to use you to bless. Start praying, now, for the people God puts on your heart. Thank Him for the strength He has given you and the opportunity you have to be a blessing to someone else.

CHAPTER 5
Some Things Are Just Sacred
(Posted May 1, 2020)

Good night. Sleep tight. Don't let the bedbugs bite. This little rhyme dates back to the 1700's during colonial times. It is commonly believed, when it was first used it was more than a simple rhyme but had meaning to the people of that day. Obviously, today it is something repeated to our children in fun. What began centuries ago as instruction is now a lighthearted saying with no significance at all.

Throughout the history of our nation there have been many things believed to be important but now we look back and wonder, what in the world were they thinking. Things like segregation and refusing voting rights to women were part of the fabric of this country for generations, but we now view these as scars and blemishes on our history. These were once the law of the land, but now the mere thought of them is repulsive to us.

Church history is not exempt from these head scratchers. We have preached and practiced many things that seemed sacred at the time but, today, we know they were man's ideas and not God's. These situations make me extremely grateful for the grace of God and our ability to learn and grow. We should always be anchored to the Word of God but always willing to walk in its light as it shines on our path.

Just as there were elements of our past that were given prominence in the church when they should not have been, I believe there are areas today that should be given high priority but—because of many different reasons—aren't getting it. Some things time and culture should not change. These are the areas that have brought us to our current existence and will need to be present if our influence continues.

This, by no means, is intended to be an exhaustive list. These are just the elements for which I feel strongly. I consider these to be "can't live without" and "protect at all costs" components of the 21-century church.

MINISTRY OF THE HOLY SPIRIT

Much can be achieved through creativity and strategy, but a serious mistake is made when we assume these can take the place of the Holy Spirit. As a matter of fact, it should be made perfectly clear that the church can only function as Christ's Body on this earth when it leans heavy on the Spirit. The church is a spiritual body; therefore, it must never try to accomplish in the flesh what was begun in the Spirit.

Unfortunately, many modern believers are spiritually anemic, and many churches are being overwhelmed because carnality has become the order of the day. My definition for carnality is, spiritual business being done in the flesh. Decisions are being made based on what feels good and fits our narrative. This always leads to frustration and defeat. The only remedy is an admission of total need for the Holy Spirit's work in all we do.

The Holy Spirit is moving right now in the hearts of His children—prompting and nudging us toward His will. We must listen and respond.

The Holy Spirit is moving right now in the life of His church—orchestrating and positioning us toward our greatest harvest. We must be sensitive and submit.

I am firmly convinced the present circumstances of our world—even though meant by the enemy for our harm—are serving as a catalyst to propel us to a season of increase and Kingdom expansion. No generation has had an opportunity like this to impact the entire globe. The Holy Spirit of the book of Acts is stirring the ashes of our hearts, reviving a flame that many thought was long gone. Something unprecedented is on the brink of happening.

We cannot let this time get by us! We cannot miss this opportunity! Our prayer must be, "O, God, we need you as never before. Fill us with your Holy Spirit and anoint us to be your people in this world." Rest assured, this is a prayer He will answer.

THE PREACHED WORD

Preaching is God's idea. I Corinthians 1:21 says, "For since, in the wisdom of God, the world through its wisdom did not know God, it pleased God through the foolishness of preaching to save those who believe." It is not just religious ritual; it is a chief tool of God to communicate His message. Preaching is important.

Styles vary. Some preachers are more polished and articulate than others. Some preachers are more demonstrative in their delivery while others are quieter and more staid. But at the end of the day, it is not the style or the ability of the preacher that matters most; it is the anointed Word of God that comes from a chosen servant of the Lord.

We, preachers, must humbly recognize the awesome responsibility that accompanies the job. When we step behind the pulpit we are representing God and speaking for Him. We must not bring reproach on Him through half-hearted sermon preparation and validating our pet peeves with "thus saith the Lord." We must approach our task with a sense of reverence and awe for the God who has called us. We carry a heavy weight.

I must confess, in my own ministry, there have been times when other responsibilities took most of my attention. These situations have moved sermon preparation to the back burner, causing my preaching to suffer. This has never been an intentional decision for me, but it has happened more times than I want to admit. Lately, I have felt deep conviction in this area. I have been reminded that my call from God was to preach. These other things—some very important—have resulted from my vocational activities or other life involvements. I know I cannot stop life from happening, but I must be intentional in protecting my call.

As a preacher of the Gospel I must:

1. Hear from God if I am going to speak for God.
2. Be thoroughly prepared to deliver a Word from God.
3. Recognize His Word is powerful; I am just the messenger.
4. Never allow my methods to hinder His message.
5. Be grateful to God for counting me worthy, placing me in ministry.

This world needs preachers set on fire by the Holy Spirit. These must be men and women of God who are not simply looking for a position but are overwhelmed with passion for the work of God. They are willing to pay the price—make the sacrifice—do whatever it takes—to take the Gospel to the world. They are consumed by the call. I want to be counted in this number.

CORPORATE WORSHIP

Something divine takes place when the people of God come together in worship. We were made for community and this is never more obvious than when we sit together in His presence. It is almost like a foretaste of Heaven when the church worships as one.

Our enemy, the devil, knows the importance of corporate worship. He has witnessed many times the fresh anointing and fierce faith that comes to believers in this holy setting. This is why he attacks this time so ferociously. He knows if he can distract and divert our attention to anything else, he can prevent us from experiencing a life changing encounter with the Holy Spirit.

Today, corporate worship in many churches is not living up to its potential. The problem is two-fold: leaders who want to showcase their talent and worshipers who refuse to participate. Both of these issues are detrimental to the health of a church and damaging to the plan God has for individuals attending that service. This subject is controversial but too important to ignore.

Worship leaders must understand this fundamental premise—their job is to lead worship. This implies 1) they are a worshiper, and 2) their goal is to bring others into the same experience. They are not entertainers. They are not concert producers. They set the table and help to create an environment where hungry seekers can experience the presence of God up close and personal. They are not the only one responsible for this experience, but they are the leader.

The individual in the pew has a key role to play in this time of worship. He/she is not a consumer. He/she is not a critic. The attitude must be that of the Psalmist who said, *"Enter His gates with thanksgiving, and into His courts with praise..." (Psalm 100:4 NKJV)* There is no need to wait until the music reaches the right speed or the song being sung is one of the favorites. The awareness of a great God who is worthy of our highest praise should be enough to take the person from spectator to participant.

When the actions and attitude of the leader on the stage and the person in the pew unite to truly worship a mighty God, beautiful things happen. This common goal overrides style preferences and brings Heaven and earth together in the room. Selfish hearts will never know this, but pure worshipers will come to church expecting it.

At the beginning of April, I had an unusual dream. I dreamed that after the corona virus quarantine ended, churches were allowed to reestablish worship times in their sanctuaries. Churches all over the country were filled with worshipers happy to be back together. That Sunday morning, the people seemed to sing with a fresh passion. Throughout the United States—in many different denominations—people worshiped with new fervor. As the people poured out their worship and praise to God, something spectacular happened—the Holy Spirit, like on the Day of Pentecost, was poured out and multitudes of believers were baptized in the Spirit. This spiritual outpouring ignited a mighty revival of miracles, sinners being converted, and the Gospel being spread in unprecedented fashion all over the world.

I woke up from this dream with a fresh hunger for a genuine encounter with the Lord. I sensed I was being reminded of the far-reaching and life changing power of corporate worship. I also felt the need to check my heart as it related to my preparation, participation and response to the worship experience. I did not want to allow my preferences, attitude or demeanor to keep me from being part of what God wanted to do. I really want to see this dream come true.

The challenges facing the church, today, are immense. Everyday there seems to be a new hurdle to overcome and a new set of concerns leadership must address. There is no joy for me in saying this, but we might as well get ready—it is not going to get easier. Great victory will always demand a high price. Fruitful ministry will always have its detractors. This is why priorities must be established and a solid foundation built. It is just a fact, in an age of change, some things cannot change.

Simply put, some things are just sacred.

AN EXERCISE IN CONTEMPLATION
Placing What I Just Read Into My Ministry Context

1. What are your takeaways from this chapter? How can it be applied to your life and ministry?

2. How important is the ministry of the Holy Spirit in your life/ministry? Can you think of times when things would have gone better had you leaned on Him instead of your own abilities? Going forward, how do you intend to be more reliant on the Holy Spirit?

3. What are the truly sacred elements of your ministry? Are there areas of your ministry that have become sacred that should not be? How do you determine what is sacred and what is not?

PRAYER ASSIGNMENT

Ask the Lord to reveal to you what is important to Him. Prayerfully and with your whole heart, commit to those things that matter to Him. Be willing to repent of the times you have failed Him but be determined to go forward with a renewed passion for His perfect will. Do not forget to thank Him for the opportunity He has given you to be involved in His work in this world.

CHAPTER 6

The Promise Is For You

(Posted May 7, 2020)

THE PROMISE IS FOR YOU

"*Most assuredly, I say to you, he who believes in Me, the works that I do he will do also; and greater works than these he will do, because I go to My Father.*" (John 14:12)

I am a firm believer in the infallible Word of God. It is a settled issue with me—if the Bible says it, I believe it. With this being said, there are some passages that cause me to wonder how they can possibly be true in my situation. The above noted scripture is one of those. I believe it, but with my weaknesses and inabilities, how can it aptly apply to me? My response to this scripture is probably not too unlike that of the disciples...

Jesus will be leaving soon. He has spent almost three years with 12 chosen men. These men have been front and center in all that Jesus did. It is going to be quite a change for them when He is gone. Jesus knows this and intentionally spends much time preparing them for life after He is no longer walking by their side. He shares with them a plan that will cause them to thrive and not simply survive.

As Jesus and His disciples are talking about their future, He lets them know His expectation is that the ministry He has begun will continue through them. He goes so far as to say to them that the works He did they would do, and their works would even surpass what they had seen Him accomplish. What a bold statement this was!

I have no doubt the disciples listened intently at every word coming from the lips of their Master. They did not interrupt Him and probably nodded in agreement—even if passively. But when He was finished, it would not surprise me if they spoke privately to each other about what they heard Him say. "Did He say what I think He said?" "Do you think He really meant what

He said, or could His words mean something else?" "How can our work ever compare to His?"

These men, whom we sometimes make heroes, were only common flesh and blood. It had to be an overwhelming thought to them that they would be entrusted with the responsibility of continuing the ministry of their Lord. Then add to this feeling those words, "...and greater works than these he will do." Well... this was just almost too much to believe. But... they knew Jesus, and they trusted Jesus, and they were willing to obey Jesus. These three simple facts/convictions would be the foundation they would stand on from that day forward.

The next few weeks would be nothing short of a whirlwind for these disciples. They watched Jesus be arrested and endure a mockery of a trial. They heard the death sentence pronounced and witnessed Jesus being brutally crucified. They saw Him die and be buried in a borrowed tomb. Three days later, they received news that the stone covering the entrance of the tomb had been rolled back, and the body of the Lord was gone. They soon discovered for themselves, the body of Jesus had not been stolen but He had risen from the dead, as He promised He would be—He was alive! They dined with the risen Jesus and went in and out of His company for 40 days. They eventually walked with Him outside the city and watched as He was taken up in the clouds to return to His Father. What a journey it had been!

Before Jesus left them, He gave some final instructions. Before they began their ministry assignments, they were to return to Jerusalem and assemble in an upper room. The instructions were to go to the upper room and wait. They really do not know what they are waiting for—all Jesus had said was, "Wait for the promise of the Father." That was not a lot of information to go on but...they knew Jesus, and they trusted Jesus, and they were willing to obey Jesus. They left the mountain from which Jesus ascended and headed for the upper room in Jerusalem.

When the disciples and other followers of Jesus arrived in the upper room—nothing happened. They took care of some business and selected a successor for Judas. And they waited. What are they waiting for? How will they know when "it" happens/arrives? How long will it be? No one has answers to these questions but...they know Jesus, and they trust Jesus, and they are willing to obey Jesus.

Then it happened! Acts 2:1-4 records it like this, *"When the Day of Pentecost had fully come, they were all with one accord in one place. And suddenly there came a sound from heaven, as of a rushing mighty wind, and it filled the whole house where they were sitting. Then there appeared to them divided tongues, as of fire, and one sat upon each of them. And they were all filled with the Holy Spirit and began to speak with other tongues, as the Spirit gave them the utterance."*

These 120 men and women assembled in that upper room will never be the same again. They are filled with boldness and the fire of the Spirit. They take the message of Jesus everywhere. They lead multitudes of people to the Lord. Mighty miracles become the expected order of the day. It is said, they turned their world upside down for Him! These common everyday men and women become world changers, and it was all made possible by three simple little facts...they knew Jesus, and they trusted Jesus, and they were willing to obey Jesus.

I love this story of Pentecost and the birth of the New Testament Church. The book of Acts is filled with accounts of the Holy Spirit and the dramatic impact He makes. Reading these accounts as history is absolutely fascinating but reading them as the beginning of the story is even more thrilling! What started in the upper room on the Day of Pentecost was not an isolated incident; it continues today!

Peter confirmed our participation in the promise of the Father when he preached his great sermon on the Day of Pentecost. His words in Acts 2:39 allow the 21st century believer to take heart and know that the same presence and power of the Holy Spirit experienced by the 1st century Christians is available to us right now. *"For the promise is to you and to your children, and to all who are afar off, as many as the Lord our God will call."* (Acts 2:39)

This reality has been experienced by many, including myself, and every day is being discovered by others all over the world. The Holy Spirit is, indeed, being poured out across the globe and hungry believers of Jesus are being baptized in this mighty river in massive numbers. He is touching people from all nations and religious backgrounds. He does not want anyone to miss this blessing.

In these unsettling times, it is good to know this wonderful experience of being filled with the Holy Spirit is available today. Just like the believers in the second chapter of Acts, one does not have to understand it or have all the facts in hand. You just have to know Jesus, trust Jesus, and be willing to obey Jesus. It is not hard or anything to fear. It is simply receiving a promised gift from God.

Do you know Jesus? Do you trust the totally trustworthy Jesus? Are you willing—with absolute abandon—to obey Jesus? If you are able to answer yes to these three questions, you are welcome to walk right into the river of the Holy Spirit and be totally immersed in His presence and power. It can happen in the sanctuary on Sunday or wherever you are right now. Just stop whatever you are doing and let the Father know you are ready to receive His gift of the Holy Spirit baptism. It is His desire to give this blessed gift to you. The promise is for you.

Normally, at this time of the year, families are gathered at local ballfields cheering for their sons and daughters as they participate in America's greatest pastime—baseball. From the little bitty guys who can barely swing the bat to the more proficient older kids, who dream about one day playing in the major leagues, everyone is enjoying participating in this wonderful sport. Unfortunately, due to the Covid-19 crisis, this part of Americana is not happening this summer or, at least, has been delayed.

If we could go watch our children play baseball tonight, there are some things we would definitely see and hear. I am confident we would hear a coach in the dugout calling for a player in the outfield to stand up and put his glove on—those outfielders have a way of becoming disengaged so far away from the action. I have no doubt some child who has just hit the ball would need to be told to run to first base—it's so easy to forget what comes next after you've focused so hard on making contact with the ball. I am absolutely certain, in every game at every level of competition, you would hear the coach say to the player, "keep your eye on the ball."

Keep your eye on the ball… This simple instruction is key to anyone playing the game. Regardless of competency or experience, success in baseball demands the player not lose sight of the ball. Injuries happen when you take your eye off the ball. The opponent gets an advantage when you take your eye off the ball. You just are not going to win if you take your eye off the ball. Keep your eye on the ball…

As 2020 was beginning, I, like many others, prayed for God to move among us in a fresh way and bring revival to our nation. I, like many others, declared this would be a year of spiritual outpouring and a great ingathering of the harvest. There seemed to be a consensus among church leaders and believers from all walks of life that this would be a time of awakening for our country. I believed it, strongly.

Then it happened...a virus began to spread across the world, infecting multitudes. Our country went on lock-down as the death toll from the virus continued to mount. Schools and businesses were forced to close, causing unemployment to reach levels near those of the Great Depression. Churches were not even allowed to meet in their sanctuaries, forcing them to create new methods to share the Gospel and do ministry. This was certainly not what anyone expected.

Then it continued...a despicable event occurred in Minneapolis as an African American man restrained in handcuffs lost his life at the hands of policemen. We all saw the video and could not believe our eyes. This event brought to the forefront again the vile spirit of racism that continues to exist in our nation. Many people responded with peaceful protests while others took to the streets with anger and violence resulting in additional deaths and destruction. This was certainly not what anyone expected.

Today I sit in my office, at the six month point on the calendar, and wonder what in the world will happen next. I continue to see the effects of Covid-19, both in the health of many friends and the economic stress in our communities. I grieve at the racial tension that remains high across the United States and my heart hurts because this issue just will not go away. The weight of both of these matters is heavy. How much more can we take? The hope of awakening and revival seems so far out of reach.

As I was praying for our country and the many people dealing directly with these two huge attacks of the enemy, the illustration I began this blog with came to mind. In my spirit I believe I heard the Lord say, "keep your eye on the ball." Somehow I believe I am being reminded that situations and events cannot stop God's plans. Through all the melee of the first half of 2020, my reaction must be that of I Corinthians 15:58—*"Therefore, my beloved brethren, be steadfast, immovable, always abounding in the work of the Lord, knowing that your labor is not in vain in the Lord."*

While we recognize the reality of the corona virus and pray for its end, and while we admit and repent of the continued existence of the sin of racism in our country and seek the reconciliation of all races, we must not take our eye off the ball. The answer to these issues and all others we face is Jesus. We must reach up to Him before we reach out to others. It is the fresh wind of His Holy Spirit that will bring us through every challenge. A genuine revival in the hearts of men and women will bring the change we need.

At this very moment—with people sick, unemployed and protesting in our streets—I still believe the rain of revival is on the way. Looking outside, I see a small cloud about the size of a man's hand and I keep getting a scent of rain. Some may think I am foolish but I'm preparing for a downpour. It is coming!

Here is what I'm going to do:

I am going to live in a state of continual repentance—meaning, I'm going to constantly be asking the Holy Spirit to keep guard over my heart. If there is any sin there—maybe way back in the dark recesses that I have ignored—I want Him to reveal it to me and forgive me of it. I do not want to harbor anything in my heart that offends my Lord. I do not want any attitude or behavior in my life that is unbecoming to a child of God. I want clean hands and a pure heart.

I am going to make prayer a lifestyle. As I stay in communication and communion with my Father, He will direct my steps, orchestrate my life and use me for His glory. This will keep me positioned to hear His voice and know His will. This will allow me to be part of the solution to the world's problems.

I am going to keep preaching truth with confidence knowing that as I plant and water, God will give the increase. I can do this even with my limited abilities because *"the Word of God is living and powerful, and sharper than any two-edged sword, piercing even to the division of soul and spirit, and of joints and marrow, and is a discerner of the thoughts and intents of the heart. And there is no creature hidden from His sight, but all things are naked and open to the eyes of Him to whom we must give account."* (Hebrews 4:12-13)

If I will live cleanly, pray passionately and preach faithfully, there are not enough powers in hell that can stop this God-ordained revival from coming!

You have got to know, our enemy, the devil, knows revival is on the way. He knows he cannot stop God but he thinks he can distract us. If he can only get us to look at the angry waves, we just might miss seeing Jesus walking to us on the water. We cannot let this happen! We will not ignore the major issues facing our world—we will confront these as the Spirit leads—but, we will not let anything keep us from the one thing this world needs more than anything else, and that is a fresh encounter with the Holy Spirit. We are determined to keep our eyes on the ball.

AN EXERCISE IN CONTEMPLATION
Placing What I Just Read Into My Ministry Context

1. What are your takeaways from this chapter? How can it be applied to your life and ministry?

2. What are some things in your life that cause you to lose focus? What are some practical things you can do to stay laser focused on your calling?

3. Are there some things you know you should have done or should be doing for the Lord, but have allowed something(s) to hold you back? What is keeping you from doing those things now? Are you willing to let the past go and get up, now, and move forward in obedience?

> **PRAYER ASSIGNMENT**
>
> Begin by repenting of the times you have taken your eye off the ball and failed to obey the Lord. Use this prayer time to start fresh with renewed commitment and determination to fulfill your calling. Ask God to help you maintain focus and recognize the distractions of the enemy. Thank Him for His patience and desire to involve you in His Kingdom work.

CHAPTER 8

More Than A Message

(Posted June 12, 2020)

Jesus is coming again. This is a message I've heard all my life. I've heard sermons, sung songs and read books on the subject. Serving many years as an evangelist, there was probably not a revival I preached that I did not address this in some way. I really do believe it—not because of all I've just mentioned but because Jesus, himself, said it. *"And if I go and prepare a place for you, I will come again and receive you to Myself; that where I am, there you may be also."* (John 14:3)

With the current distress and upheaval in the world, the subject of the second coming of Jesus is getting a little more widespread attention than it has had in recent years. I'm seeing a lot of social media posts and memes pointing to, what some feel, is the beginning of the end times. This is usually the case when bad things happen—people, especially religious people, begin to talk about the end of the world. I'm not being critical, just pointing out facts as I see them.

Sometimes I wonder if we really believe He is coming soon. Is this just a fall-back subject when things happen we can't explain? Is this just "church speak" when we are afraid and the ugliness of sin is rising to the top? I wonder, if we really believed Jesus was coming again, if our business as usual would change. I wonder…

This morning in prayer, my attention was drawn to a passage of scripture found in Ephesians. Talking about the Church, Paul wrote, *"That He might sanctify and cleanse her with the washing of water by the word, that He might present her to Himself a glorious church, not having spot or wrinkle or any such thing, but that she should be holy and without blemish."* (Ephesians 5:26-27)

Paul described the Church for which Jesus would be coming back. He said His bride would be a glorious church without spot, wrinkle or blemish and that she would be holy.

HIS CHURCH WILL BE WITHOUT SPOT

I think He is saying she will be without sin. This thought moves me to a place of genuine repentance. I don't want any sin in my life to separate me from the Lord. The pleasures of sin exist for a season but the price we pay for them is far too great. I pray for the washing and cleansing work of the Holy Spirit in my life. I want all of my sin covered by the blood of Jesus.

HIS CHURCH WILL BE WITHOUT WRINKLE

Sitting too long cause wrinkles in garments. Fatigue and worry cause wrinkles in complexions. Could my inactivity cause me to be wrinkled? Could my armchair quarterbacking, while my brothers and sisters are in the heat of the battle, cause me to be wrinkled? Could my weariness and worry actually be lack of trust in God and cause me to be wrinkled? These are questions that deserve an answer. If we really believe Jesus is coming soon we might want to take them seriously.

HIS CHURCH WILL BE WITHOUT BLEMISH

This is interesting. Unless Paul is just being repetitious, he is making a distinction between spots and blemishes. I looked for the dictionary definition of blemish. It says a blemish is, "a small mark or flaw which spoils the appearance of something; a moral defect or fault." I believe this deserves a deeper look.

I wonder if long-held unholy attitudes could be considered blemishes? I wonder if deeply ingrained feelings toward people—maybe other races and ethnicities—could be blemishes? I wonder if preaching against some sin while ignoring other sin could be a blemish? I wonder if determination to have my way instead of submitting to His will could be a blemish? I wonder if we would prefer not to think about this at all? I wonder...

HIS CHURCH WILL BE HOLY

I think this means His church will look like Him, act like Him, think like Him, and totally reflect Him in all it does. It can't be driven by personal agendas—it must be His agenda. It can't belong to a man—the righteousness of all men is as filthy rags in the sight of God. It isn't working to keep people out—it is feverishly working to bring all people in because it is not God's will that any should perish. When the world sees the church, it must see Him.

The church described in Ephesians 5 is the church for which He is coming. He will not be grading on the curve and He is not looking for the best three out of four. He expects us to be without spot, wrinkle, blemish and to be holy. These are our guideposts and instructions as we prepare for this blessed event. We must heed them without exception.

One more time, I want to go on record as saying I believe Jesus is coming again. The message I was taught as a child and the one I have believed and preached throughout my ministry is more true today than it has ever been. The signs are all around us. Read the Bible and watch the news—it is really pretty clear. But somehow, this Biblical truth has got to be more than a catchphrase—it has to affect my living. I can't be scriptural in speech and unscriptural in practice. The message of the Lord's return calls for action on the part of the people of God.

What should my personal response be to the message of the second coming of Jesus?

It should cause me to guard my heart. I will not live a life of condemnation, but I must live one of deep conviction. I can't allow anything to enter my life that will offend my Lord and separate me from Him. I am responsible for myself, therefore, I will be a vigilant watchman over my heart.

It should cause me to be sensitive to the Holy Spirit. I refuse to become hardened and stubborn toward the Holy Spirit. I want to be soft and pliable—always willing to be corrected by Him. I don't want to become a spiritual elitist—I want to walk humbly before my God. I don't want to demand my rights—I want to take up my cross and follow Him. If I am going to live in the Spirit, I want to walk in the Spirit. As He leads, I will follow.

It should cause me to pursue intimate communion and communication with the Father. I want to be with Him. I need to hear from Him. I don't know the way—the challenges are too great for me—I'm helpless on my own—I really need the Lord. Communicating and communing with Him is more than an event, it must be my lifestyle.

It should cause me to be passionate about the harvest. I can't sit back and watch the world go to hell in a hand basket. I can't just shake my head as the world burns around me. I can't be critical when a sinner sins, for had it not been for the grace of God I would be there with them. I must engage in the harvest. I can't win everyone; I can't fix everything, but I can do something. There is a ripened harvest with my name on it—I must go get it.

I don't know how much time there is before Jesus comes again. There have been a lot of date setters throughout history and they have all been wrong. The early church expected Him in their lifetime. My parents expected Him in theirs. I'm looking for Him in mine. The fact is, no one except the Father knows when it will happen. I am just certain of this one thing—He is coming. This truth must be proclaimed but it must also be lived. I want to be ready and I want to reflect it in my daily walk. I want His coming to be more than just a message.

AN EXERCISE IN CONTEMPLATION
Placing What I Just Read Into My Ministry Context

1. What are your takeaways from this chapter? How can it be applied to your life and ministry?

2. Do you believe Jesus is coming again? Does your service reflect your belief in this message? How should this message affect your life and ministry?

3. Do you know people who are not prepared for the return of the Lord? If so, what are you doing about it?

PRAYER ASSIGNMENT

Pray the message of our Lord's return will come alive in your spirit, leading you to stay prepared and motivating you to actively engage in the harvest. Pray specifically for unsaved friends and loved ones. Pray God will use you to bring lost people into the fold before His return. Be sure to thank the Lord for your salvation and for the opportunity He has given you to participate in His end-time plan.

CHAPTER 9

Revival...Will We Know It When We See It?

(Posted July 8, 2020)

I grew up in a small town in southeastern Oklahoma in a vastly different era of time from today. Instead of computer games, we played real games. My adventures were limited only to my imagination. Every day I was outside with my friends and oh the fun we could have with the simplest of things!

One of the most exciting games we would play was racing our bicycles down Red Hill. Red Hill was this very steep mountain a few blocks from my home. It rivaled Pikes Peak in its height. The kids in my neighborhood and I would push our bikes up that gigantuous incline and race each other to the bottom. The key was to never touch the brake—that was real adventure! As a ten-year-old boy, I literally took my life in my hands with that daredevil feat. It is a wonder I survived.

A few years ago—after telling this story to my family many times—I took them to see Red Hill. I really do not know what happened. That huge mountain was gone, replaced by a small hill. The place of so many of my boyhood near-death experiences was not what I remembered at all. I have got to tell you, my stories of grand conquest over an enormous challenge lost its luster. Reality was not what I recalled at all.

I have noticed, many times in life we paint pictures in our minds of how certain things were or should be, only to be disappointed when we discover reality. Sometimes this can be as amusing as my example. Other times, we can miss the joy of the real by holding onto the imagined. It is healthy to dream but it is important to be able to process those dreams through reality. I want to be a man of big dreams, but I do not want to be a man who lives in fantasy.

LEADERSHIP THOUGHTS

Today in the church there is much talk about revival. I am one of those who believe we are on the brink of a spiritual outpouring. I sense a stirring in my spirit that is unlike anything I have ever felt before. I, like many others, believe God is about to do something truly spectacular in the earth. The question is—will we know it when we see it?

Having spent all my life in a Pentecostal church, I have read about and witnessed many moves of God. I have seen many people set free and delivered from the shackles of sin. I have seen many people healed of all manner of sickness and disease. I have seen God answer prayer by making a way where there did not seem to be one. I have seen God move in His power and demonstrate His great glory. These experiences have shaped me and made me the man I am today.

But I have been wondering, is what I have seen what God wants to do again? Is what is coming simply an updated version of what we have already had? Could it be possible that what God has planned will look quite different than our past experiences? Could my expectation, based on my experiences, cause me to miss what God has planned? Could I really miss the revival God is sending because I am looking for something else? Will I recognize this revival when I see it?

I am seriously considering these questions in my own life. Recently in prayer, I believe the Lord brought to my mind five characteristics of the revival He is sending. I will not take the time to elaborate on each of these in this blog—that may come later. Here is what I believe a last-day revival is going to look like:

- It will not be a public relations opportunity for a church or an evangelist but a total shift to Jesus.
- It will not just produce converts but disciples.
- It will not just be a spiritual outpouring but radical transformation.

- It will not produce programmed benevolence but a lifestyle of servanthood.
- It will not be an event but a revolution.

This looks like far more than I have experienced in my lifetime. This seems to go much deeper than a Jericho march and an extended altar call on Sunday night. These characteristics will not automatically occur in a prayer line. I like Jericho marches, extended altar calls and prayer lines—these have been genuine elements of past moves of God and may still be again—but world changing revival is more than this. I do not want my memory of what was to keep me from the reality of what God wants to do today.

I am concerned many churches—especially classical Pentecostals like myself—could miss what God is doing while waiting for something else. We know what God has done but to stretch and go further requires risk we are unwilling to take. But deep inside I sense the Holy Spirit is saying, "relax and follow me." This next revival may not look like yesterday's, but it will be what we need to cover the globe with the Gospel and usher in the return of Jesus. This revival may look different, but it will make us more like Him.

Our world has plunged into utter chaos. Things are so broken, neither a Democrat nor a Republican can fix them. The downward spiral has become so drastic, conversation and meetings cannot stop it. Vaccines, stimulus checks or legislative action will not bring about the change for which the masses are calling. I have come to the conclusion, revival is the only thing that is going to help—not the revival I remember, nor the revival in which I have become comfortable, but a revival that shakes us to our core and transforms us fully to the Church for which He shed His blood.

You may ask, "how can this happen in my church?" This answer is simple. Any church—large or small, city or rural, young or old—that is willing to pray until it happens and not settle for anything less will see this revival. The moves of God of the past will pale in comparison to the far-reaching transformative revival that is on the way. You can be part of it!

Revival is coming! The question that must be answered is—will you know it when you see it? I am determined to be prepared and spiritually sensitive to what God is doing. I will not try to bind Him to my preference or tradition. I will take the reins off and say, "Holy Spirit, move as you will." I will not miss what He has reserved for this last day.

AN EXERCISE IN CONTEMPLATION
Placing What I Just Read Into My Ministry Context

1. What are your takeaways from this chapter? How can it be applied to your life and ministry?

2. How do you define revival? What are some characteristics of revival? Have you, personally, experienced revival? What needs to happen for genuine revival to come to your life and ministry?

3. Is it possible, preconceived ideas of how revival should look can hinder the revival God wants to send? Are you willing to step out of your comfort zone in order to receive the revival God wants to send to you? Do you want revival in your life and ministry enough that you are willing to do whatever it requires to have it?

PRAYER ASSIGNMENT

Pray for revival in your life, family, church, and world. Be willing for the Holy Spirit to show you areas of your life that could be used to delay or interfere with the revival He wants to send. Repent of these areas He reveals to you. Make yourself available for Him to use. Give God praise for the promise of a last-day outpouring of His Spirit.

CHAPTER 10

The Spotlight Keeps Coming Back To Me

(Posted July 31, 2020)

How much more can we take? I am ashamed to admit, this is a question I have asked several times over the past few weeks. The prolonged crises happening in our nation seem to have no end. They are striking so close to home and leaving an imprint that will remain forever. I am tired, and long for the days I remember not that long ago. I just want things to be normal again.

When our world turned upside down earlier this year, I felt—and even said—this, too, shall pass. I genuinely believed our issues would be dealt with, and after awhile, we would carry on—hopefully better and stronger. My optimistic self believed we were strong enough to address wrongs and big enough to defeat enemies. We have been challenged before—we will overcome as we always have. But I am sitting here today wondering when it will ever end.

I am praying. I am praying for the President, Congress and Courts. I am praying for groups that have risen in our county who hate our way of life and seek to destroy us from within. I am praying for medical personnel and researchers who are dealing with the pandemic. I am praying for media who stoke my fears. I am praying for those who are truly hurting and are victims of all that is taking place. But I need to be honest…the more I pray, the more I feel the spotlight shining back on me and my church. I just do not feel He is finished speaking to and working on us.

I love the church. I still believe it is the Body of Christ on this earth. It is the Bride of Christ that will soon be caught up together to meet Him in the air. It is built on the rock and all the powers of hell will never prevail against it. The true church of Jesus Christ is, indeed, alive and well. But…I am wondering if there is more I need to do to align with His church. I am wondering if, during my stewardship, I have strayed from His original intent. I am wondering if this season is an opportunity for me to adjust my sails and get it right. I am wondering...

Over the past many years I have witnessed what I call the Americanization of the church. In many cases the Apostolic voice is missing and we operate by what we think and feel. We demand a vote on everything so our voices can be heard. We talk more about our rights than we do His will and Word. Self-promotion and posturing have replaced prayer, and a seat at the table has become more important than time in His presence. We have become program driven instead of Spirit led. We view the church no differently than any other organization in the world. We have moved so far from the New Testament church we were birthed to be. Could this be part of our problem?

I do not speak for anyone else, but I believe we have drifted. We are busy with good works but we remain anxious and anemic. We do love Jesus but we are easily distracted by the angry waves around us. We continue to preach the Word but our belief is sadly mixed with unbelief. The passion with which we began the race has slowly lost much of its fervor. The movement is becoming an institution.

In Luke 24, there is a story of two men who at one time had great hope that change was coming to their world, but because of the death of Jesus, this hope was lost. They are walking home from Jerusalem when, unbeknownst to them, Jesus appears and walks with them. As they discuss the events of recent days, Jesus engages with them in conversation but they still do not recognize Him.

These men finally arrive at their home and, because of the late hour, invite Jesus to spend the night with them. As they begin to eat supper together, Jesus blessed the food. The scripture tells us, it was at this time their eyes were opened and they recognized Him. Jesus immediately vanished from their sight.

Many of us can relate to the overwhelming disappointment the two disciples felt in the beginning of the Luke 24 story. We began 2020 with declarations of revival and awakening, but before much of the year is gone, we are unable to meet in our church facilities because of a pandemic, and cities throughout the nation are burning. Unemployment and business closures have skyrocketed. We have witnessed despicable acts of hatred and injustice in our streets. We are watching politicians in Washington sacrifice our country because of their feelings toward their opposing political party and leaders. On and on it goes.

But, just as we relate to the disappointment of the disciples, let us not forget Jesus is still walking with us! Somehow, I must push through my circumstances and connect with my resurrected Lord. I want what happened in this story to happen to me.

HIS WORD BURNED WITHIN THEM

After Jesus departed from them, the two men recall their time with him on the road. They said in Luke 24:32, *"...Did not our hearts burn within us while He talked to us on the way and while He opened the Scriptures to us?"*

I want holy heartburn again! Like the Prophet Jeremiah, when I feel like quitting and I think my work does not matter, I want His Word in me like fire in my bones. Nothing can take the place of His Word. I need the strength, instruction and power of the Word in my life. I must give priority to His Word in all I do. I must have it!

THEY INVITED JESUS INTO THEIR HOME

Home is where you are who you really are. There is no pretense at home. Into this most intimate place, these men invited Jesus.

If I am going to be who He has called me to be, I must take Jesus home with me. He must be welcome in my private places. He must be part of my discussions and plans. The effectiveness of my public ministry will be determined by my private moments with the Lord. The days of making backroom plans without His direction, and expecting God to be good with it, are over. Jesus must be welcome at all times in all places.

THEY HAD TO SHARE THE GOOD NEWS

When it was revealed to the disciples it was Jesus who had been with them, they quickly returned to Jerusalem to give the news to all their friends. They could not keep this information to themselves. They had to share it!

I cannot become paralyzed by fear, intimidation or anything else. The Gospel must be preached—in the church, on the internet, and through every avenue of media. It must be shared in the neighborhood, in the workplace, and on the street corner. My friends and family must hear it. People I have never met have got to be told. In a world looking for good news—I have got some! I have got to tell it!

In these chaotic times, I know there is an answer for the church. But I hope someone hears this—we cannot proceed with business as usual. Systems that have worked for us in the past will not pull us through these challenges. Marketing and slick presentations will result in frustration. If we listen closely, I believe we will hear God say, "You've tried your way, now it is time to try mine."

What is God's way? His way is for the priests to weep between the porch and the altar. His way is for the call to go forth for a solemn assembly. His way is for judgment to begin at the house of the Lord and for His people to repent. His way is for our idols to be destroyed and for Him to be the Lord of our lives once again. His way is for us to seek Him and His Kingdom first—then those other things we need will be given to us.

I believe there is a cure for Covid-19 and an answer for every other issue troubling us today. I believe the outpouring of the Holy Spirit, we have been expecting, is still coming. I am still anticipating a mighty awakening in this nation and a sweeping revival across the globe. In reality, everything happening causes me to believe these things even more—the devil as a roaring lion is pulling out every stop to prevent it but he cannot do it! I believe!

But I remind you—we must do things His way.

"When I shut up the heaven and there is no rain, or when I command the locusts to devour the land, or send pestilence on My people, if My people, who are called by My name, will humble themselves and pray, and seek My face and turn from their wicked ways, then I will hear from heaven, and will forgive their sin and will heal their land. Now My eyes will be open and My ears attentive to the prayers of this place." (II Chronicles 7:13-15)

LEADERSHIP THOUGHTS

AN EXERCISE IN CONTEMPLATION
Placing What I Just Read Into My Ministry Context

1. What are your takeaways from this chapter? How can it be applied to your life and ministry?

2. Have you ever been disappointed in your ministry? If so, how have these disappointments affected your faith? What are some things you have done—or should do—to overcome and move past your disappointments?

3. Do you believe you have a role to play in what God wants to do in the world today? Are you willing to be a catalyst for positive change in your world?

> **PRAYER ASSIGNMENT**
>
> Be willing to repent for drifting from God's plan, and recommit to submitting fully to His will. Seek Him for clear direction for your life and ministry and express your desire to follow Him, regardless of what others do. Do not forget to praise Him for the honor He has given you in allowing you to be part of His plan in these times.

CHAPTER 11

I Am Human But I Am His!

(Posted September 24, 2020)

As a God-called preacher of the Gospel, I always walk through my storms unfazed and every time I come out of a fiery time of testing you cannot even smell smoke on my clothes...wouldn't it be great if this were true? The truth is, all of us, regardless of our standing and relationship with God, find ourselves from time to time in places that seem overwhelming. We can put on our best face but deep down inside we are anxious ,and concerns about our survival cannot be denied. Here is the deal—no matter how long you have been a Christian, you are still human. Tough times are part of life.

The disciples learned this fact to be true one night while sailing across the Sea of Galilee with Jesus. Their assignment was to transport the Lord to the other side of the sea while He rested after a busy day of ministry. They are experienced and well-equipped for the task, so what could go wrong? And, besides all this, Jesus is on board the ship with them.

Sometime during the night a great storm arose. The wind is boisterous and the waves are high. The boat is violently reeling back and forth and is taking on water. The disciples are doing the best they can to keep the ship together, but it appears in spite of their best efforts, the ship is being destroyed and they will most certainly go down with it. You have got to know they did not see this coming!

Finally, after what may have been hours fighting this storm, one of the disciples asked the question, "where is Jesus?" He certainly was not helping them in this crisis. They were doing all they could to keep the ship from coming apart, but Jesus was totally uninvolved. As they began to look around—sure enough—they found Jesus where He had been all along—in the back of the ship fast asleep.

LEADERSHIP THOUGHTS

One of the men cried out in desperation, "Lord, get up and help us! We are dying! Don't you care?" Jesus got up and, in a calm resolute manner, looked at the situation and said, "peace, be still." Immediately, the wind stopped and the sea settled down.

I love this story because of all the practical truth it contains. You would think the primary take-away from this lesson would be—the great faith of the disciples moved Jesus to respond with a miracle. This, however, is in no way the case. As a matter of fact, the disciples seem to be operating in fear, not faith. They did not cry out to Jesus saying, "Lord, we know you are all-powerful. Help us in this situation." Their actual cry was, "Lord, help us. We are about to die!" They have heard His sermons, seen His miracles and love Him enough to leave all they have to follow Him—yet, in this storm they are afraid.

If that storm caused the humanity of the disciples to be displayed, I probably should not be so hard on myself when events in my life cause mine to show. I love Jesus and am fully committed to serving Him, yet, sometimes...sometimes I am afraid...sometimes I am overwhelmed...sometimes there just does not seem to be a way out. I have watched Him move for me countless times, but this storm just feels different.

Times like these cause me to relate to the man in Mark 9 who came to Jesus with a great need. Jesus said to the man, "if you can believe, all things are possible." With tears streaming down his face, the man replied to Jesus, "Lord, I believe. Help now my unbelief." I think the man was saying, "Jesus, I know you have all power—in no way do I doubt your ability. I'm just wondering if you're going to help me." He knew Jesus could, but he wasn't sure Jesus would.

It is very important to note, in both of the stories I have referenced in this article—the disciples in the storm and the man with a great need—Jesus intervened and gave a miracle. He did this, not because of great faith, but because of His great love for His children. This Father and son/daughter relationship trumps everything else! Jesus really does love us!

This truth became very clear to me many years ago when my daughter, Kristina, was moving into her first apartment while a student at Lee University. Donna and I were helping her get the apartment set up when I decided I should take her to the grocery store. I wanted to make sure, before we left to go home, she had everything she needed.

Kris and I—along with her ridiculously small list of grocery items needed—headed to the supermarket. As I pushed the cart down the store aisle, we passed many things I knew she liked but were not on her list. I would point these items out to her and ask if she wanted them. Each time she would reply, "Daddy, I don't really need that right now." I would say, "but I know you like it. You always eat this when you come home. Let's just get a little." This scenario repeated itself over and over. I was having the best time shopping with my little girl and getting her all the things I knew she enjoyed.

It was not until we got to the checkout line that it reality hit me! As I watched the number getting larger and larger on the cash register, I realized Kris probably did not need all of those things right now...but it was too late. I pulled out the American Express and paid for all the fun I had just had!

Now you can believe this or not, but right then and there—in the grocery store checkout line—the Holy Spirit spoke to me. He said to me, "You've had a good time today giving your little girl things you know she likes. If you then being earthly know how to give good things to your child, how much more will the Heavenly Father give the Kingdom to them who ask Him!" He let me know He delighted in blessing me even more than I delighted in blessing my daughter!

You and I find ourselves, today, in some pretty difficult times. A virus is raging throughout the world, bringing fear, disruption and destruction with it. Our political landscape has become acrimonious and bitter. Forces are at work to divide our nation along racial, philosophical and economic lines. Our enemy, the devil, is surely at work.

Many are facing intense personal battles. Sickness, loneliness, fear…on and on the list goes. These are not figments of our imagination—these problems are real and they hurt really bad. To make matters worse, when we come to these times in our lives, there is that accusatory voice in our mind telling us, "this wouldn't be happening to you if God really loved you. You aren't worthy of His love." We have all been there—some reading this are there right now.

I am so happy to have this opportunity to share some good news with you! Regardless of what you are feeling and how bad you are hurting, Jesus loves you and will not forsake you because of your situation. As a matter of fact, He wants to draw nearer and prove to you He is your answer. He will not run from you—He is running to you! You are His child—He is your Father! You may not feel like a person of mighty faith and power—that is ok. Just come to him as you are. He will not turn you away.

"Come to Me, all you who labor and are heavily burdened, and I will give you rest. Take My yoke upon you, and learn from Me. For I am meek and lowly in heart, and you will find rest for your souls. For My yoke is easy, and My burden is light." (Matthew 11:28-30 MEV)

The devil tells me I am just a human without rights and without hope. I tell the devil he is a liar—I am a human but my Father is the King! I am human but I am His!

AN EXERCISE IN CONTEMPLATION
Placing What I Just Read Into My Ministry Context

1. What are your takeaways from this chapter? How can it be applied to your life and ministry?

2. Have you ever been hesitant to call upon the Lord for help when you were facing a problem of your own making? How does recognizing God as your Father change the situation? Is there anything for which your Father will not help you?

3. Make a list of some storms you have faced in life. Beside this list, make another one showing how God brought you through that storm. How does this exercise affect your faith? Do you believe God will intervene in your present storm?

PRAYER ASSIGNMENT

Spend a good deal of time praising God for the many storms He has brought you through. With great confidence, take your needs to Him knowing you are His child, and He is your Father. Thank Him, by faith, for the answers that are coming.

CHAPTER 12
Awakening Is On The Way

(Posted October 22, 2020)

Anticipate. The dictionary gives multiple definitions of this word, some of which are: to regard as probable; to be aware of (what will happen) and take action in order to be prepared; and to look forward to. This word has played into my life many times in many ways.

I remember as a child anticipating special events like Christmas, birthdays and that last day of school before summer break. I remember anticipating my 16th birthday knowing the first order of the day would be a trip to the DMV to get my driver's license. I remember the anticipation I felt those few days before November 25, 1981, when I knew my life would change forever (for the better!) as Donna would become my wife and we would be a family. I remember anticipating the birth of our daughter, Kristina, and the many joys she would bring to our world. It seems so many of the big important events of my life have been preceded by a season of waiting with expectation—anticipation.

There was never any doubt these things would happen but that did not change the fact I had to wait and, in many cases, make preparation. My patience was sometimes tested but when the time was right, it happened.

This lesson must not be lost in the realm of the Spirit. As believers, we learn to pray and wait. During our time of waiting we grow and receive revelation. Our prayers are not futile religious exercises—they are bathed in faith and rooted in God's Word. As this process is taking place, we look forward to the response of our Father—we anticipate His answer.

For a long time, many of us have been praying for an awakening in our nation. We have watched the moral decay and the downward spiral of our society. We have seen the overt effort to remove God from the public square. We have seen the desensitization of the populace and their willingness to accept sin as normal. We have witnessed all of this yet believed at some point the wind of revival would blow again. At times it has not looked promising—it has even seemed impossible—but we have kept on praying...and anticipating.

I know some will say I am foolish for writing this. Others will think I am giving in to wishful thinking. Disbelief has always existed and certainly abounds in many today, but...my spirit is rising within me in anticipation of a great outpouring of the Holy Spirit in our nation and around the globe. I believe God has heard (and is hearing) the cries of His children and His promise to pour out of His Spirit in the last days is about to happen! My heart is burning within me with anticipation!

Throughout its history, the United States of America has played a major role in what God has done in this world. It was not a mere coincidence that a small group of people sailed across the Atlantic Ocean toward the New World in 1620 seeking religious freedom. These pilgrims had no idea what their landing at Plymouth Rock would begin. A nation would be born that would be a lighthouse for freedom to the entire world and assume the lead in taking the Gospel to the four corners of the globe. Anyone who tries can see, despite egregious sin and error on the part of many, God has greatly used this country.

I do not believe God is finished with us yet! I know we have failed Him. I know great injustices and much evil are present. I get it—God is in the business of building His Kingdom and not the systems of men. I know God is not an American. But... there remains a strong presence of His Body in the nation and until we are taken away He will be working.

The call goes out, today, for the Church to assume its position and prepare for what is coming. We must be a unified Body—not a white church/black church; not a conservative church/

progressive church; not a traditional church/modern church. We must be His Church—washed in His blood, filled with His Spirit and committed to "go into all the world and preach the Gospel to every creature." We cannot let any distraction keep us from His charge. The Church in this country must come together and lead the way in an awakening that will shake the very foundation of this world.

How can this happen? Well...it is really not that difficult. We make it complicated by our opinions and endless analyses. We feel the need to create strategies and programs. Under the guise of finding consensus, we study until we stall and nothing gets done. It is probably time to simplify and return to some basics. Here are my thoughts...

1. PRAY

We know how to do this. We may have to return to an old-fashioned concept of tarrying, but we know how to do this. We know how to pray until we pray through. We know how to pray until we get into a spirit of prayer. We do not need a manual or a workshop—we just need to pray. Let's not complicate things—let's pray.

Revival will come to America when we pray. This revival will spread throughout the world when we pray. *"...For My house shall be called a house of prayer for all nations."* (Isaiah 56:7)

As we commit to prayer, the Holy Spirit will begin to speak to us. He will lead us into truth and give us direction. He will convict us of sin and reveal iniquity within us. If we respond as we should, this will move us to the next important step.

2. PREPARE

This is where personal responsibility comes into play. We accept that as sure as some things can only be done by God, some things God expects from us. Our attention to the Holy Spirit's directives aligns us with His will and allows us to participate in the divine plans He has for our country and world.

The last days will be marked by a fresh wind of the Spirit. Structures and systems that cannot accommodate this will need to be changed. This will not be change for change's sake; it will simply be an adjustment of our sails in order to be moved by the Holy Spirit. The praying Christian who has prayed through self, tradition and the world will understand this and willingly do it. The carnal Christian who chooses to give lip service to preparation will miss it. The choice is really that simple.

I am convinced from the Word of God, a large part of our preparation must be repentance. *"For the time has come for judgment to begin at the house of God; and if it begins with us first, what will be the end of those who do not obey the gospel of God?"* (I Peter 4:17)

Repentance has been a popular subject in recent years as prominent leaders have led us in repenting for the sins of our nation. While I believe this is good and necessary, I caution the believer lest you feel this alleviates the need for personal repentance. I am repulsed by abortion, human trafficking, social injustice and so many other sins in our nation and I know God is as well. But...we will be in a much stronger position with God when we first deal with our own sin. Pride, prejudice, cheating, lying, sowing discord, secret sin we think is hidden...on and on the list goes—these sins cannot be glossed over. Personal repentance must take place and will be a huge element in our preparation process. When we come clean before God and turn from our sin, He will hear our prayers and heal our land.

"Righteousness exalts a nation, but sin is a reproach to any people." (Proverbs 14:34)

3. ANTICIPATE

When we pray and prepare—get ready! Our Father who loves us more than we can possibly understand is so ready to respond to us with his absolute best. *"If you then, being evil, know how to give good gifts to your children, how much more will your Father who is in Heaven give good things to those who ask Him!" (Matthew 7:11)*

It is not a matter of if; it is a matter of when. We understand His response will come in His time. We wait…but we wait with expectation. We anticipate any day now the answer will come.

God is a man of His word. *"Heaven and earth will pass away, but My words will by no means pass away." (Matthew 24:35)* He will do what He said He would do. It is time to stand up straight, square our shoulders and look resiliently toward the heavens. Our answer is on the way!

Now I need to say something that must be heard—our enemy, the devil, will not give up easily. He has a chokehold on many areas of our country and he will not let go without a fight. Even recently as we have begun to see the possibility of some positive breakthroughs to some longstanding problems, he has reared his ugly head and gotten in the way. Riots in the streets, deep division in government and a deadly virus that disrupted every area of our society are just some examples of his intrusion. Expect more to come.

The devil will fight but we will win! We will win if we pray, prepare and anticipate. There is no question about it. Hold on to this and fight back from a standpoint of victory. *"Yet in all these things we are more than conquerors through him that loved us." (Romans 8:37)*

I am not ashamed to tell anyone I love my country. I still get a lump in my throat when I stand at a ballgame with my hand over my heart and hear the national anthem. I still believe God brought us into existence for divine purpose. I still believe

He wants to use us in this world. I still believe revival is near. I have not lost hope. I still believe.

It may not come like we thought it would. God may use people we would not expect Him to use. All of that is all right with me. I will leave the details to God and fully trust His plan. I am just hungry for revival that stretches from coast to coast and spreads to every nation of the world. You may say it cannot happen. I say, just watch! I am anticipating!

AN EXERCISE IN CONTEMPLATION
Placing What I Just Read Into My Ministry Context

1. What are your takeaways from this chapter? How can it be applied to your life and ministry?

2. What lessons have you learned while waiting? Are you in a time of waiting now? If so, what do you feel the Lord is saying or wanting to show you during this season?

3. What is your role in the coming revival to our country and world? What is the role of your church in this revival? Are you being faithful to your assignment?

PRAYER ASSIGNMENT

As you begin your prayer, ask God to show you how He sees you. Be willing to repent of any sin or area of shortcoming in your life. Pray for your family, church, and community. Sincerely ask the Lord for His will to be done on earth as it is done in Heaven. Thank God for all He has done but do not forget to praise Him for all He is about to do.

CHAPTER 13

Your Church— A Lake Or A River?

(Posted November 30, 2020)

A A couple of mornings ago as I was praying, the Lord showed me something I feel I need to share with you. I saw a beautiful river as it flowed through the countryside. It flowed for several miles, then all of a sudden, it reached a place where there was a logjam in its path. This logjam was strong enough to all but stop the flow of this river—only a few small streams were able to penetrate it.

Interestingly, at the place of the stoppage, a large lake had developed. This lake was beautiful in its own right. The lake was surrounded by rich vegetation. People would come and go enjoying the lake. I saw different kinds of wildlife come out of the nearby wooded areas to drink from the lake. It was obvious this lake, that had been created by the river water unable to break through the logjam, had become an accepted fixture in this community. Much pleasure was gained by the creation of this lake.

As I was seeing this flowing river, stopped by the logjam creating a lake for people to enjoy, I heard the Lord say, "This is, sadly, the church in many places."

I have not been able to get away from this vision. The words said to me by the Lord were not spoken in anger but in disappointment. It seems He was saying His plans for us are far greater than we are experiencing. I believe He was saying we have settled for much less than He has prepared for us.

Too many churches have chosen to be a lake instead of a river. A lake can definitely meet a need. A lake is usually the focal point of a community and a place to be celebrated. Most people enjoy a lake. But...your church is not called to be a basin filled with water; you are called to be a flowing river bringing life to everything you touch. You are not simply a meeting place for Christians to enjoy; you are a mighty river meant to affect every aspect of culture. You are the living, breathing Body of Christ in this world!

Satan recognizes the potential of the Church. He has created this logjam with the intent of stopping the river. He is not threatened by a religious institution that meets together a few times a week and reaches out to the needs of a community, much like any other civic organization. He must feel good when he can disrupt the flow and cause us to be satisfied with maintaining the lake.

Sadly, I see this happening today in too many places. We are preoccupied with disputes with each other, arguments over style and methods, and disagreements over texts that have nothing to do with our salvation. We agree the world is in trouble, but developing a plan to do something about it is a task for another day. We keep the lake looking good but that logjam is still stopping the river.

The time has come for an identity check in the church. We need to remember the words of our Lord in Matthew 16 when He said, this is His Church and the gates of hell cannot prevail against it. We need to remember the authority He said we had in verse 19 of this chapter, *"And I will give you the keys of the Kingdom of Heaven, Whatever you forbid on earth will be forbidden in Heaven, and whatever you permit on earth will be permitted in Heaven."* (Matthew 16:19 NLT) This does not sound like a passive, "take it as it comes" body; this sounds like a difference-making, life-giving movement! This is who we are created to be!

We become this Church when there is:

LESS EMPHASIS ON GROWTH AND MORE EMPHASIS ON HEALTH

Our goal is not building a big ministry; our goal is becoming everything God has called us to be. Growth will naturally happen when good health exists.

LESS EMPHASIS ON PROGRAMS AND MORE EMPHASIS ON POWER

If programs could change the world we would not be in the shape we are in. Programs can be helpful tools but it will take the power of the Holy Spirit to impact our world. *"...Not by might, nor by power, but by my Spirit, saith the Lord of hosts." (Zechariah 4:6 NKJV)*

LESS EMPHASIS ON PERFORMANCE AND MORE EMPHASIS ON PRODUCTIVITY

What difference does it make if we have all the bells and whistles in our worship services but the Kingdom does not experience increase? These times call, not for a high-tech performance but an encounter with a risen Savior. We must bear fruit that remains.

LESS EMPHASIS ON WHAT FEELS GOOD AND MORE EMPHASIS ON WHAT DOES GOOD

It has almost become a cliché—church is not about us. Somehow this must be more than words; it must become our life theme. We are not looking for a feel-good experience; we are a militant body moving throughout the world, reclaiming territory stolen by the devil. We are active, aggressive and victorious!

LESS EMPHASIS ON RELATING TO THE CULTURE AND MORE EMPHASIS ON CHANGING THE CULTURE

We are *in* the world but not *of* this world. We are the called-out ones and being different is not something to avoid but something to embrace. We are here to reflect Jesus to a fallen world—that requires we be more like Him and less like them. We are salt and light in the world. When we take this responsibility seriously, a positive difference will be made.

The time has come for the logjam to be removed and the river to flow mightily through the world. This will only happen when we earnestly seek God for fresh anointing—the kind that breaks every yoke. As we pray and seek Him, He will reveal to us those things that must change to loosen us from bondages and free us to rise up as the army of the Lord. The time has come...the time is now!

The words Jesus spoke to His disciples in John 14 resonate in my spirit as I write this. *"Most assuredly, I say to you, he who believes in Me, the works that I do he will do also; and greater works than these he will do, because I go to My Father. And whatever you ask in My name, that I will do, that the Father may be glorified in the Son. If you ask anything in My name, I will do it."* (John 14:12-14 NKJV)

A lake church reads this and moves on. A river church reads this and says, "Yes, Lord! Let it be done in me!"

We have arrived at an exciting time for those who are tired of religious activity and are hungry for a divine move of God. Promises like those in John 14 were not placed in the Scripture for our reading pleasure; they are intended to be a reality in our lives/ministries today. This truth is setting people free and taking many to a fresh season of the miraculous. Breakthrough is happening. Barriers are being broken.

God is calling you to leave the lake and get back in the river. His plans for you are greater than mere survival. His will is to thrust you forward—past every hindrance—to a place of awesome fruitfulness. It can happen. It will happen. I believe I can even say, it is happening!

Dear God, I am hungry. I am tired of religious activity. I want to go deep in you. I want my church to be a city on a hill and alive in the power of your Spirit. I want to see the promises you made to me in your Word become a reality in my life and ministry. I want to change my world for your glory. I surrender fully to your will—I hold nothing back. Change me. Fill me. Use me. Take me where I have never been. I am ready, Lord. Do it today. In Jesus name, I pray. Amen

LEADERSHIP THOUGHTS

AN EXERCISE IN CONTEMPLATION
Placing What I Just Read Into My Ministry Context

1. What are your takeaways from this chapter? How can it be applied to your life and ministry?

2. Is your church a lake or a river? Do you feel any responsibility in this answer? What can you do to ensure your church is strong and healthy?

3. What is your church doing, now, to impact your community and advance the Kingdom? Is there anything you can do to make your church more effective? Are you willing to do it?

PRAYER ASSIGNMENT

Spend some time thanking God for your church and the opportunities it has been given to make a difference in the world. Pray for a fresh wind of the Holy Spirit to move through your church, taking it to new heights in Him. Ask God to remove any hindrances that are keeping you from going forward. Make yourself available for Him to use to accomplish His plans. Begin to praise Him for the revival heading your way.

CHAPTER 14

Keeping The Faith On Saturday

(Posted January 14, 2021)

The scene at Calvary was excruciating. The mother of Jesus and a few of His followers sat and watched all that transpired. I cannot imagine the sorrow and grief they experienced through the whole ordeal. That had to be, without a doubt, the darkest day of their lives—they watched Jesus suffer and die.

The words of a couple of the disciples, on the way to Emmaus three days after the Lord's death, summed up the feelings of hopelessness felt by all those who trusted Jesus. *"The chief priests and our rulers delivered Him to be condemned to death, and crucified Him. But we were hoping that it was He who was going to redeem Israel…" (Luke 24:20-21 NKJV)* They had such high hopes for Jesus…but He died.

Jesus was taken from the cross and placed in a borrowed tomb. The people returned to their homes…grieving, confused, and afraid. In spite of all that Jesus had done to prepare them for this time, they did not seem to know what to expect next. It is going to be ok—as a matter of fact, it is going to be great—but you could not tell it by anyone's actions. All present evidence points to defeat. It simply appears all hope is gone.

As bad as Friday was for the followers of Jesus, Saturday was a whole other story. They have cried all they can cry. The heart-wrenching grief they felt at the cross has turned to numbness. The questions now focus on what we do next. Preparation is being made for their life after Jesus. There seems to be no thought of what will happen the next morning. We know how this story ends, but those living it do not see a good conclusion at all.

Well…early the next morning—the third day—the miracle of all miracles occurred at the tomb. Just like He promised, Jesus rose from the dead! He proved death could not hold Him. He showed all the world He had all power in Heaven and earth. He also showed His disciples He was a man of His word, for He had told them much earlier, *"...Destroy this temple, and in three days I will raise it up."* (John 2:19 NKJV) Jesus kept His promise!

I have got to tell you, there have been many times I have lived out the truths of this story in my own experience. I have had those Friday experiences when my dreams died only to be followed by Sunday when resurrection occurred. When I tell my story, it usually has two components—Friday's trial and Sunday's victory. But what about that day in between? I do not talk much about Saturday.

The truth is, Saturday is very important to my story. I would even say finding my victory on Sunday is dependent on how I live out my Saturday. No matter how bad Friday was, I will never make it to my triumphant Sunday if I give up on Saturday. I must keep the faith on Saturday.

Saturday is when I accept the fact I have done all I can—there is nothing left for me to try. Saturday is when I put everything in the hands of the Lord—I place my full trust in Him. Saturday is when my trust in God calls for me to rest in Him—I simply wait for Him to perform His will. Saturday is not a day to lose hope—it is actually when hope is incubated to become faith. Faith is developed on Saturday.

So…here you are. You have prayed and claimed the promises. You have fought hard and done everything you know to do. You really thought your answer would have been here by now, but it has not come. You are tempted to throw in the towel and accept the fact it is not coming—it must not be the will of God. But hold on just a minute…it is just now Saturday! Sunday is resurrection day, and it is not here yet. No matter what you see, how you feel, or what they say—God will keep His promise to you. Do not give up on Saturday!

Here is the plan the devil does not want you to know. It works every time. This is what we will call the Strategy for Saturday.

REST IN THE LORD

The battle has been long and hard. You have fought valiantly. You have kept fighting and believing when many others have quit and walked away. You are tired. Your exhaustion is causing you to let your guard down, and doubt is beginning to creep in—not intentionally, but it is happening nonetheless. It is time to retreat to the arms of the Father and let Him hold you for a while. This is not giving up—it is being refreshed and strengthened. It is in this moment of stillness that revelation will come to you.

"Be still and know that I am God; I will be exalted among the nations, I will be exalted in the earth. The Lord of Hosts is with us; the God of Jacob is our refuge. Selah." (Psalm 46:10-11 MEV)

LISTEN TO THE HOLY SPIRIT

There are many voices clamoring for your attention. Listening to all the chatter of this age will simply frustrate and confuse you. Peace and revelation come when you listen to the Holy Spirit. He will guide you into truth and lead you on a right path. He will settle your spirit and restore your joy. He will come alive in you, replacing your weakness with His power. Get in the Bible and let the Holy Spirit speak to you!

START EXPECTING VICTORY

Your Friday experience is not the end of your story. It looked bad…it was bad! Your hurt and disappointment are real. The report you have been given does not lend itself to much hope. But…it is just Saturday—Sunday is coming! Here is what separates the believer from the unbeliever—the unbeliever sees facts that say, it is over; the believer gets facts from the Word of God, which declare, it is not over until God says it is over. Choose to believe the report of the Lord and start expecting your victory!

You will be able to keep the faith on Saturday when you rest in the Lord, listen to the Holy Spirit, and start expecting victory. That is a pretty good strategy by which to live your life.

I have vivid memories of a time of great stress and battle I faced as a college student. I loved the Lord with all my heart and did my best to serve Him, but this did not stop the attack of the enemy upon my life. I wanted very much to find my place in God's plan, but it seemed everything I tried ended in frustration. I remember feeling pretty tired and weak.

Early one morning, the phone in my dorm room rang. I answered to the voice of a dear lady in my church who loved me and had taken me under her wing. After some very brief pleasantries, she got to the purpose of her call. I'll never forget her words to me, "Les, I was praying for you this morning. The Lord told me I should call you and direct you to a verse of Scripture. I am at work right now, so I do not have time to discuss it—we will talk later. I just want you to go and read Philippians 1:6."

I immediately picked up my Bible and found the verse to which my dear friend had directed me. *"Being confident of this very thing, that He who has begun a good work in you will complete it until the day of Jesus Christ." (Philippians 1:6 NKJV)* I began to tremble as I felt the Holy Spirit speaking directly to me. I read and reread that verse. I wrote it on a piece of paper and placed it in my wallet. I memorized it. This was a Word from the Lord to me, and I was not letting it go!

That day—and today—this verse told me, regardless of my present situation, God had begun a good work in my life. It also told me, regardless of my present situation, the work He had begun would be completed and there was nothing the devil or anyone else could do to stop it. I believed it then, and I believe it now!

Many reading this right now find themselves in a place of stress and trial. It looks like the promise has died and all hope is lost. You are hearing some experts tell you, it is impossible—it is over. Your flesh is reminding you of what you witnessed Friday—it is hard to see any good come from that. Logic tells you, giving up is your best option. But…I remind you, your Sunday has not gotten here yet. Do not quit now—you must keep the faith on Saturday. Your Heavenly Father will not fail you. He will see you through. He will complete what He has started in your life..

LEADERSHIP THOUGHTS

AN EXERCISE IN CONTEMPLATION
Placing What I Just Read Into My Ministry Context

1. What are your takeaways from this chapter? How can it be applied to your life and ministry?

2. What are you waiting on God to do? How do you cope with a delayed answer? How could the Strategy for Saturday, in this chapter, help you?

3. Do you have a favorite "go-to" Scripture from the Bible? Write that verse here and commit it to memory.

> **PRAYER ASSIGNMENT**
>
> Use this time to remind yourself of the greatness of God and the fact that He is much bigger than the problem you are facing. Begin to audibly claim promises in His Word that speak to your situation. Tell God exactly where you hurt but also let Him know you trust Him fully. Ask Him for revelation and rest. Praise Him for all He is doing and will do in your life during this season.

CHAPTER 15

A Safe Place To Turn Around

(Posted March 5, 2021)

Not too long ago I found myself on a narrow two-lane road on my way to an appointment. I had never been in this area, so I was trying to be careful and watch for the place I needed to turn. But, as happens to me occasionally, I did not see the sign for my turn in time to make it, so I had to keep driving. I wanted to just stop and make a U-turn but there was no shoulder to the road and there was the occasional car coming from the opposite direction, so I knew that was not a good option for me.

I could tell the car driving behind me knew the area and was becoming frustrated at my hesitant speed. They could not pass me, so they had to just slow down and follow. Being aware of their presence caused stress for me but I could not move over and did not intend to miss an opportunity to turn around.

As I continued to drive, I was very conscious of the fact I was going farther and farther from my desired destination. I was also mindful of the time—I had somewhere to be, and I did not want to be late! I am sure my blood pressure was rising as all these factors began to add up. I needed to do something, but I had to be careful. I had to keep going until I found a safe place to turn around.

This real-life story reminds me of the challenges all leaders will face multiple times, as they navigate the minefield of change in the group they are called to lead. You feel you know where you need to be as a group/organization/church but being able to get there will not always be easy. A sudden turn—a quick decision—a careless move—can be catastrophic. The key to successful change will always be finding a safe place to turn around.

Change is inevitable. It occurs whether you want it or not. Our human bodies are the best examples of change. Look at a picture of yourself from ten years ago, then look in the mirror. Notice anything different? You have changed! Regardless of your diet, exercise regimen and mental fitness you cannot keep change from happening. Change is a natural part of the process.

The world around us is changing. Sometimes I reminisce about the world in which I grew up, causing me to feel somewhere along the way I was transported to another planet, because the world I live in now in no way compares to the one of my childhood! I did not ask for these changes, but they happened, nonetheless. As is often said today—it is what it is. Change just keeps on coming!

Very few people are surprised at the changes from the two examples I just gave. We may not like it, but we accept—and even expect—these changes. But...change within the group—especially the church—is another matter entirely. I change, my world changes, but leave my church alone! But guess what, change happens at church, too. We must keep the same message, but methods will need to change from time to time.

What are some things to remember when entering a season of change? I am sure this is not an exhaustive list, but here are four statements I believe any leader needs to consider when approaching change:

CHANGE MUST BE LED

Leaders must be intentional with change. There always should be a clear understanding of the reason, process and target of the change. Communication with the group will be extremely important—there should be no surprises. Surprises breed suspicion. Suspicion causes trust to be lost.

Even when change takes place incrementally—which in many cases is the best policy—someone needs to own it and be responsible for keeping everything on track. Leaving anything to chance is a dangerous course to take. As the cliché' goes—failing to plan is a plan to fail. There can always be adjustments to the plan but there must be a plan.

Leaders earn their stripes during seasons of change. Standing at the helm puts one in a vulnerable position, but that is when leadership must rise to the occasion. There will be times when patience must be exercised. There will be times when decisions must be made. There will be times when you swim against the current. There will be times momentum is on your side and times when it is not. During the good, the bad and the ugly—leaders lead.

THERE CAN BE A WRONG WAY TO DO THE RIGHT THING

I have worked with many pastors who told me they were confident they heard from God on a matter. Despite this firm conviction, their efforts failed. Their heart was right and their motives were pure but, still, things did not work out. In many of these instances the change that was sought was noble but the plan to achieve it was lacking.

There is a classic example of the wrong way to do the right thing in I Chronicles 13:7-11. In this story David and his men are bringing the Ark of the Covenant back to Jerusalem after it had been stolen and removed by the Philistines. A plan is devised to place the Ark upon a cart to be pulled by oxen—what could possibly go wrong?

As this celebrating caravan make their way toward Jerusalem, the oxen stumble and the Ark shakes. Uzzah, caring deeply for the security of the Ark, reached out and grabbed the Ark simply to stabilize it. This actually seems like a good thing to do—but there is a problem. God had strictly forbidden anyone to touch the Ark. When Uzzah did this, he was immediately struck dead. God's response to Uzzah's action tells us there can be a wrong way to do the right thing.

I am grateful that, unlike Uzzah, our mistakes will probably not bring sudden death to us, but they can bring much frustration and disappointment. This is the reason leaders must pay attention to details. While most of us are goal oriented, the path leading to the goal is of utmost importance. Never ignore the process. How you achieve your goal does matter. The end does not justify the means. When you get to where you are going, you want to feel good about how you got there.

Here is a nugget to remember—a leader's integrity will be affected more by the *how* than the *what*. The systems of men reward the result while the hearts of the people are changed by how you achieved the result. Good leaders care about those they lead. Manipulative leaders use people to gain advantage for themselves. Choose to be a good leader with unblemished integrity.

SAFE ARRIVAL AT YOUR DESTINATION MUST BE A PRIORITY (CRASHES CAN REALLY RUIN A GOOD DAY!)

We have often heard about those who win the battle but lose the war. This happens when shortsighted leaders only see what is immediately in front of them but fail to consider what happens next. These situations rarely end well. There is momentary gratification but the pain that follows is greater than the preceding joy. This problem is taken off the table by a clear understanding of the big picture and making sure each step taken leads to the desired destination.

Leaders must never be so sure of their "rightness" that they develop a "win-at-any-cost" attitude. The desired change may be in the best interest of the group but until the group believes this—or is at least willing to try—the changes are good for no one. Remember the goal is safe arrival at the destination with as few casualties as possible.

Too often the battlefield of change resembles the battlefield of war—casualties and destruction everywhere. The leader made the changes desired, but the price was great. The thrill of victory is hollow because the losses will be hard to overcome—if they ever can be.

There is a simple fact to keep in mind when the possibility of change is being explored—everything we do in life has a price attached. What will the price be to make the change? What will the price be if we do not make the change? Is the difference between action and inaction great enough to merit the change? It is a very foolish leader who will not take the time to sit down and count the cost before launching into drastic change within any organization.

Sometimes you just have to go for it. The group is heading in a disastrous direction, and waiting for a better time to institute change is not an option. This is a tough predicament in which to be, but these situations do exist. But even when this is the case, a good leader will go the extra mile to avoid crashes. Safe arrival at the destination for all the people is the desired outcome.

ABORTING A PLAN IS NOT ALWAYS BAD

Football fans know that sometimes the best play for your team is to punt. Punting the ball to the other team means you are giving up on your present set of downs but with the expectation of getting the ball back in a better position. We do not score this time, but we look forward to another opportunity.

Sometimes plans do not work. Sometimes timing is just not right. No matter how we frame it, push for it and believe in it—it ain't happening! When this happens, a wise leader backs up and makes a new plan. Continuing to fight a losing battle makes no sense; living to fight another day makes all the sense in the world. Aborting the planned change in this situation is not loss; a dogged determination to have it your way, regardless of the cost, will bring great loss. Leaders need to know how to punt.

This article began with me driving down the road needing to turn around but unable to do so. It was necessary for me to continue driving away from my desired destination in order to find a place where I could turn around safely. I was frustrated—drivers around me were angry—people expecting me wondered where I was—but none of that mattered. The success of my trip required me to stay the course until I found a safe place to turnaround.

Sincere leaders are always looking for ways to make things better and to become more productive. Most usually it will be determined change is necessary for this to occur. There will be many opinions as to what these changes should look like and when they should happen, but the leader—while listening to the advice of others—must make a thorough survey of the landscape and make the best decision possible. Much will be involved in this decision, but it all begins with a single turn. Be careful—be wise—be prayerful. Make sure you find a safe place to turnaround.

AN EXERCISE IN CONTEMPLATION
Placing What I Just Read Into My Ministry Context

1. What are your takeaways from this chapter? How can it be applied to your life and ministry?

2. How comfortable are you with changing ministry methods in your church? What are some changes you feel would be helpful in making your church healthier and more impactful?

3. What are some practical steps to lead healthy change in your church? What are some pitfalls to avoid? What role are you willing to allow the Holy Spirit to take in the process of change in your church/ministry?

PRAYER ASSIGNMENT

Pray earnestly for sensitivity to the Holy Spirit's direction and the needs of the congregation, as you lead through this season of change. Ask God to help you see His plan and seek Him for a strategy to implement it. Be willing for the Holy Spirit to change your own plans as you submit to His. Give Him praise for all He is doing and even more praise for where He is taking you.

CHAPTER 16
It's Harvest Time!
(Posted May 5, 2021)

There is nothing more important to a farmer than harvest. It is the culmination of all his efforts. He has withstood the freezing temperatures early in the season, the excess rains in the spring and the scorching sun of the summer. He has overcome the insects, weeds and wild animals that preyed on his crops. Now, waiting in the field, is the fruit of his labor. The harvest is ready!

Everything has been leading up to this time. Many people would have given up. Many would have considered the challenges and never gone to the trouble to even plant. But the experienced farmer had the hope of harvest. It was this hope of harvest that kept him going. Now he is rewarded.

There are very few events in nature that have greater spiritual application than that of the harvest. For many years we in ministry have been sowing seed. We have had many obstacles to work through—it has not always been easy. Some gave up but many kept plowing the fields and planting the seed. We have sown and watered, believing one day God would give the increase. The hope of harvest has not let us quit. And now...it is harvest time!

As we approach this most critical time, there are three truths that must not be forgotten: harvest is urgent; not all harvest is ripe; and the neglected harvest will be lost.

HARVEST TIME IS URGENT!

Nothing can stand between the farmer and the harvest. There may be other things that need to be done but they will have to wait—it is harvest time. Next week may be a more convenient time but that is too bad—it is harvest time. The farmer may wake up with a headache and sore throat, but he will just have to work through it—it is harvest time. Every excuse—regardless of its legitimacy—will have to be ignored. The harvest demands full attention. It will not wait for anything.

Growing up in the southwestern part of the United States, I have visited many little sleepy towns during wheat harvest. I have watched those towns that normally roll up the sidewalks at 6 o'clock every evening come alive when it is harvest time. Every motel is full and RVs are parked everywhere they can be. People from all over the country have been hired and brought in to help bring in the wheat. Late into the night you can hear the combines humming in the fields. Business really picks up during harvest season!

The reason for the sense of urgency is well documented. Harvest time is also storm season. Everyone in the region knows to keep an eye on the sky. They know weather conditions can change very quickly. A severe storm can wipe out, in just a few minutes, everything the farmer has worked months to accomplish. This realization calls for an "all hands on deck—we've got to get it done" attitude. Veteran farmers are serious about the harvest.

This is exactly the truth Jesus was trying to communicate to His disciples concerning the spiritual harvest in John 4:35 when He said, *"Do you not say, There are still four months and then comes the harvest? Behold I say to you, lift up your eyes and look to the fields, for they are already white for harvest."* You can hear the urgency in His words—the harvest is ready. He even says it is past ready. Jesus is saying, there is no time to wait—it is harvest time!

Before a full appreciation for the harvest can be experienced by today's church, a genuine sense of urgency must take over. For many years, we have been teaching evangelism and developing strategies to win our cities for Jesus. At some point we must leave the pew and the classroom and move to the streets, neighborhoods and marketplaces. While we say, there is four months before the harvest, Jesus is saying, the fields are already white for harvest. We cannot keep seeing the harvest as an event to come; it must become an assignment to complete.

NOT ALL HARVEST IS RIPE

As I am writing this blog, I am very aware, throughout my community many people are actively involved in planting vegetable gardens. In a few weeks, these gardens will begin to produce a wonderful array of vegetables that will grace dinner tables, be shared with friends and neighbors (of which I hope I will be a part!), and stock freezers to be enjoyed later in the year. This really is my favorite time of the year!

A simple truth every gardener knows is—everything in the garden does not ripen at the same time. A tomato plant, today, may have multiple green tomatoes on it but only one that is red. The gardener will harvest the red one and come back tomorrow to see if others are ready to be picked. Harvest is a developmental process—you wait for it to be ready.

This principle must not be lost as we consider the spiritual harvest. Not everyone is ready at the same time. The key is not to lose the ripened harvest while waiting on a desired harvest to become ripened.

Many times, there are those dear to us we so desperately want to see saved. We witness to them. We pray for them. We do everything within our power to win them to the Lord, but they do not respond. What should we do when this happens? Keep witnessing, keep praying, keep doing everything within your power to win them to the Lord, but... do not miss others around you who are ready while you work on someone who is not. Don't give up on anybody...but don't overlook that one God has put in your path who is ready right now to accept the Lord.

The prayer of the soul-winner must be, "Lord, make me sensitive to the ripened harvest. Lead me to those who are hungry to know you. Don't let me overlook any soul you place in my path."

Now, please hear me—this act of responding to the ripened harvest does not mean you are giving up on your unsaved loved ones. I believe this is an instance where God's laws of "give and it shall be given to you" and "you reap what you sow" will come in. While you are allowing the Holy Spirit to use you to bring to faith someone you may not even know or have relationship with, He will be moving on the heart of your loved one. They may not be ready today but hold on! The harvest in your home will come in!

THE NEGLECTED HARVEST WILL BE LOST

I learned this lesson many years ago at my one and only attempt to have a small garden. I broke up a little area of ground behind our house and planted a few tomato and pepper plants. I did my best to take care of them until it came time for our family vacation. We were away for just over a week. When we returned, the weeds in the garden were green, but my plants were not. The little bit of fruit on the vines had withered and was worthless. My little garden had died because of my neglect.

It is a simple fact—there is a shelf life for the harvest. As I have already mentioned, it will not wait for us and it will not last forever. There is a short time span for reaping. If you miss this time, the crop in the field is lost forever.

This truth must resonate in the spirit of every believer. We may have the best of intentions and a well-thought-out evangelism strategy. However, we keep postponing the launch into the harvest, waiting for various tasks to be completed and other things to fall into place. But just remember, while we are waiting, souls are dying. The neglected harvest is lost.

I remember hearing a song in church when I was a little boy titled, "Harvest Time." It was written in 1949 by a lady named Wanda Smith. The chorus reads,

Harvest time, harvest time,

The grain is falling, the Savior's calling;

Oh, do not wait! It's growing late,

Behold, the fields are white, it's harvest time.

We sang that song like we meant it and if it was true then, it certainly must be true now. There is a ripened harvest all around us. I do not want to lose my harvest because of my neglect.

I began this article by saying, nothing is more important to the farmer than the harvest. I want to end it by saying, nothing is more important to Jesus than the harvest. Jesus came to this earth "to seek and to save that which was lost." His death on the cross was not about changing history; it was about changing eternity—changing eternity for everyone ever born. Nothing means more to our Lord than souls.

Brothers and sisters, we have been talking about this day for a long time. We have been planning, praying and working. The hope of harvest has been motivation for us. Some gave up, but we did not. Some will not see it, but we do. Some may miss it, but we will not. This is our time—this is our moment. God has brought us to the Kingdom for such a time as this. We will not fail.

It is harvest time!

LEADERSHIP THOUGHTS

AN EXERCISE IN CONTEMPLATION
Placing What I Just Read Into My Ministry Context

1. What are your takeaways from this chapter? How can it be applied to your life and ministry?

2. In those moments when you are tired and want to give up, what keeps you in the race? Who in your life is watching you that you must not fail?

3. How important is the harvest to you? Who do you consider to be your harvest? What are you doing to reach your harvest?

PRAYER ASSIGNMENT

According to Matthew 9:38, we are to pray to the Lord of the harvest to send laborers into the harvest. Do that now. Pray for God to raise up individuals with a heart for the harvest and ask God to let you be one of those. Earnestly pray for your lost friends and loved ones to come to accept Jesus. Pray for an awareness and sensitivity to the ripened harvest all around you. Spend time praising Him for the ingathering of souls that is coming to your ministry.

CHAPTER 17

What We've Got Here Is Failure To Communicate

(Posted June 4, 2021)

I thought it was a pretty simple order—a cappuccino and two regular coffees. This is the order I made at Dunkin Donuts on a recent visit to Boston. Donna said the cappuccino was perfect; Kristina and I were not as pleased with our coffees. For some reason, the young man with whom I placed the order made a mistake and added cream and sugar to our coffee—this was not alright. We wanted black coffee—you know, regular coffee.

Very kindly, I made my way back to the counter to exchange the coffee I did not want for what I had ordered. I explained to the young man I had ordered regular coffee but had been given coffee with cream and sugar. His quick response to me was, "You aren't from here, are you?" I immediately thought we were about to have a conversation about my accent (which happens at least once a day when I am in this part of the country!) but actually I was about to be taught a lesson on ordering coffee in Boston. I was told regular coffee there means cream and sugar is added. Who knew?

Obviously, this was not an issue to argue over, so I accepted the mistake was made by me. I must admit, however, I was fairly certain the guy at Dunkin was telling this southern boy a big story to cover his error. As soon as we got back in the car I googled, "ordering coffee in Boston" and, guess what—he was telling me the truth! Lesson learned!

In this instance, no one was really wrong. I placed my order just like I had done hundreds of times back home. The man at Dunkin Donuts prepared my order just like he had done hundreds of times in his store. What I meant and what he heard were two different things entirely. The problem was simply one of communication.

As one who has spent much of the last 43 years speaking in public, I am always looking for ways to improve my ability to communicate. As a preacher, I am very aware that delivering a sermon is one thing but communicating a message is another. I have not succeeded by completing my sermon—my success is reached when those listening to me truly get it. Proper response to my sermon will only be achieved when there is a clear understanding of what I am saying.

Whether you are a preacher, teacher or parent talking to your children—whether you are the foreman on your job, candidate running for office or coach of your church softball team—whatever you are and to whomever you are speaking, good communication will be key to your success. The speaker and the listener must be on the same page. Failing to do so leads to consequences no one wants.

In order to become a good communicator, I believe there are four essentials to which a speaker must commit. This is not a pick three out of four, it is all or nothing. Here are what I feel are the non-negotiables in communication.

KNOW YOUR AUDIENCE

The mistake I made in Boston happened because I assumed my audience there was just like my audience in Cleveland, Tennessee. This assumption on my part led to some really bad coffee! If I had known my audience from the outset, I would have known the word to use was black not regular.

Knowing to whom you are talking allows you to speak the language of the room and avoid those mistakes that sabotage what you are trying to accomplish. Will they understand your joke? Will they understand your euphemisms and slang? Will your method of communicating enhance or distract from your message? A little pre-thought can make all the difference in the world in your outcome.

RESPECT YOUR AUDIENCE

No one enjoys being talked down to. So much more can be accomplished in a communicative setting when both parties have mutual respect. The responsibility for ensuring this mutual respect is solely in the hands of the speaker.

The two elements for conveying this respect will always be approach and attitude. I must show respect from the very beginning and maintain respect throughout the entire discourse. A speaker who fails to display these traits will be limited in effectiveness. Depending on the audience—some may receive a little, while most will totally turn the speaker off and not hear a word. When this is understood and the goal is good communication, respect for the audience is accepted as imperative.

LISTEN TO YOUR AUDIENCE

I have come to the conclusion that some speakers really enjoy hearing themselves talk! They drone on and on without any consideration of how what they are saying is being received. In many of these instances, the listener gave up long before the speaker did, resulting in very little being accomplished. If the goal was saying a lot—mission accomplished! If the goal was communication—total fail!

This issue can be avoided by giving some time to listening to the audience. The last thing a speaker wants to do is answer questions no one is asking. Gaging the level of interest and determining the ability to understand can only be learned by listening. Communication is, indeed, a two-way street. Good communicators understand that speaking is only half of the process—listening is extremely important.

LEADERSHIP THOUGHTS

LEAVE SOMETHING WITH THE AUDIENCE

Have you ever sat through a presentation and, when it was over, wondered, "What in the world was that all about?" All you knew was, that was an hour of your life you would never get back! There were a lot of words that came out of the speaker's mouth but nothing to take home. This is not good communication.

When a speaker knows, respects and listens to their audience it should not be too difficult to find enough content that can be deposited into the heart of the listener. It is here when the speaker moves beyond the ear and enters the heart that communication takes place that has a lasting impact. This is the crowning achievement of the speaker—knowing that information was imparted and will be remembered.

As I am writing this blog, I cannot help but remember that famous line in the classic movie, Cool Hand Luke. When Captain is having a hard time getting rebellious Luke to follow instructions he says, "What we've got here is failure to communicate." Luke discovered in very explicit ways the horrendous consequences that come from poor communication.

I do not expect our audiences to be placed in solitary confinement because of our failure to communicate, but it is very disappointing when the message we feel is important enough to share is not received by those to whom we are speaking. It would seem to me, if the message matters, we should want to do our absolute best to ensure it is heard—not just heard with ears but with heart.

Even though we have advanced technology to assist us, there has never been a time in history when true communication is as difficult to achieve as it is today. Distractions, limited attention spans, entrenched ideologies…the list is quite long of the challenges in conveying a message. This is all the more reason we must be intentional in our preparation to speak and sensitive to the many factors taking place while we are speaking. We cannot take anything for granted.

I am determined to be a better communicator. I believe in my message; therefore, I am committed to making sure it is packaged in a way that it will be heard and remembered. I want to say what I mean and help my audience completely understand.

I do not ever want a regular cup of coffee again!

AN EXERCISE IN CONTEMPLATION
Placing What I Just Read Into My Ministry Context

1. What are your takeaways from this chapter? How can it be applied to your life and ministry?

2. What are some potential problems that could interfere with your ability to communicate with your audience? What is your plan to overcome these hindrances?

3. Which is more important to you—delivering your message or communicating your message? If communication is your goal, how will you know if it is achieved? What are you doing to improve your communication skills?

PRAYER ASSIGNMENT

Begin by thanking God for entrusting an important message to you. Ask Him for a special anointing to communicate this message. Ask Him for creativity to develop your presentation and sensitivity to your audience. Be willing for Him to show you areas in your delivery that need improvement. Ask for help in making these changes. Pray and believe the next time you speak will please the Lord and be a blessing to those who hear you.

CHAPTER 18

God Is Speaking—Are You Listening?

(Posted September 16, 2021)

I have always been a big fan of radio—especially AM radio. I remember, in my younger days, enjoying running the dial late at night to see all the far away stations I could pick up. Depending on the weather conditions, the dial would be filled with "in and out," "staticky" stations from all over the country and even one from south of the border. I admit it didn't take much to amuse me as a child and this activity would do it every time.

Radio waves are very interesting to me. Just think—right now, bouncing off the walls of the room where you are reading this, are radio waves from all over the place. You don't hear them because you don't have a receiver. If you will get a good receiver and tune it to the proper frequency, you'll be amazed at what you will hear. The sounds are present, but an activated receiver tuned to the right frequency is required to hear them.

There is some definite spiritual truth in the aforementioned example. I have no doubt God is speaking to His Church today. The question is—are we in a position to hear Him? He is speaking—He has been speaking for a long time—but unless we are a tuned in receiver, we will not hear Him.

I must admit there are times I am not tuned in. It is sometimes a challenge to move past the many distractions of our day to listen intently to the Holy Spirit. We want to hear Him—we know we need to hear Him—but so many things are vying for our attention. Speaking for myself, an intentional decision must be made to get in the closet (whatever this is for you) and get down to business with the Lord. He is never far away. I just need to focus…and listen.

I had one of those times earlier this week. I knew perfunctory prayer and devotions would not be enough. I needed a Word from God and nothing else was going to satisfy. I did what I have done many times throughout the years—I took my Bible and notepad to my quiet place and prepared for an encounter with the Lord. After a little while, it happened. The Holy Spirit began to speak, and I heard.

Among several things I believe the Lord spoke to me on this particular day were the following instructions to the church as it relates to positioning ourselves for what He wants to do among us in these important times.

There is no doubt in my mind God is moving across the world, today, with a fresh wind of His Spirit. This is not an isolated move of God; this is a global move of God. His promise to pour out of His Spirit on all flesh is truly being fulfilled and will only become more prevalent in the coming days. These are exciting times, indeed, to be part of His Church!

But the sad reality is, many will miss what God is doing. Because of a myriad of reasons—religious spirits, tradition, lack of vision, secret sin, unbelief—to name a few. Some will watch as the revival touches and transforms others but they, themselves, will not be affected. What a tragedy this is!

This does not have to be your story! You—your church—your ministry—can move from the bleachers onto the playing field. You can be right in the middle of all God is doing. You do not have to be a spectator; you can be actively involved and here is how:

WAKE UP!

The day of the sleepy, passive Christian is over. While we were sleeping, the enemy crept in and took our nation, many families and, sadly, many churches. We slept and he stole. We were very comfortable while we slept—we even enjoyed beautiful dreams. But while we were sleeping and dreaming, destruction was occurring all around us. It is time to wake up!

A big part of being awake is being aware. So many have adopted the philosophy of, ignorance is bliss. As long as we do not know about it, we are not responsible. This attitude is an affront to everything the Body of Christ stands for. We are not a people who runs and hides from the crisis; we are the ones who have been called to storm the gates of hell and demand the enemy to let go! We pray for the Holy Spirit to sharpen our vision to see the needs around us and we boldly go where He leads us. We are awake and vigilant!

The cry of the Lord through the prophet Joel is a call to the church today, *"Proclaim this among the nations: Prepare for war! Wake up the mighty men, Let all the men of war draw near, Let them come up."* (Joel 3:9 NKJV)

This is the time for all hands on deck. Sound the alarm! Wake up!

MAKE UP!

It pains me to say this, but some will miss what God is doing because of division, hard feelings and verbal assassinations within the church family. Jealousy of other ministries and personal/political agendas that hurt people have become far too common within the Body. It seems an end-time strategy of the devil is to divide and cause us to turn on each other. In too many places he is having overwhelming success.

One of my favorite verses in the Bible is Psalm 133:1—*"Behold how good and how pleasant it is for brethren to dwell together in unity!"* This unity does not mean sameness or conformity. It means we are all in the same boat together, rowing in the same direction and working for the same cause. We are together even though we are not all alike. We can celebrate each other and recognize each member has an important place and responsibility in the Kingdom. We are not threatened by each other; we support each other and welcome to the table every brother and sister in the Lord.

This unity must become a treasured and protected element in our church. Infighting and distrust will cripple us. Someone must be big enough to say, "I am sorry." Someone must be strong enough to say, "I do not want to hear it." Someone must be spiritual enough to say, "I forgive you." It is only when we are willing to come together, in a genuine spirit of unity, that we will see God's best manifested among us.

Now here is a word to the wise—in the real world, offenses will arise. You are going to get hurt at some point—it will happen. These are times not to sow disparaging seed but to show grace, extend mercy and reflect Jesus. You can speak against systems, decisions and actions but attacking a brother or sister personally is actually an attack against the Father. Believe it or not, the Father loves the offender just as much as He loves the offended. You can be sure God, in His own way, will take care of an erring child. Leave that to Him.

"Therefore if you bring your gift to the altar, and there remember that your brother has something against you, leave your gift there before the altar, and go your way. First be reconciled to your brother, and then come and offer your gift." (Matthew 5:23-24 NKJV)

SHOW UP!

Great victories are available for the believer, today, but you must be present to win! Sitting in the corner and watching the world go by—and complaining about it—is not the position to which we have been called. It may feel safer to shelter in place, but the prize goes to the one who leaves the bunker and enters the arena. We have to show up!

There has never been a time when it has been more important for the church to make its presence known, than today. We need involvement in every area of life. We don't just need preachers in the pulpit—we need Spirit-filled believers in seats of government. We don't just need worshipers in the sanctuary—we need strong believers in Hollywood, on Broadway and in Nashville. We don't just need teachers in Bible college and seminary—we need committed followers of Jesus on every school campus. We don't just need Christians in church on Sunday—we need disciples of our Lord to infiltrate the marketplaces and every area of society. We need to leave the fort and move into battle!

"You are the light of the world, a city that is set on a hill cannot be hidden. Nor do they light a lamp and put it under a basket, but on a lampstand, and it gives light to all who are in the house. Let your light so shine before men, that they may see your good works, and glorify your Father in heaven." (Matthew 5:14-16 NKJV)

SPEAK UP!

Bullies love to intimidate, and the devil is a big bully! He is working to intimidate the church into silence. If we speak up, we will offend. If we speak up, we will run people off. (And here's a big one.) If we speak up, we will lose our tax-exempt status. I think you will agree, we hear these things all the time.

I have never liked bullies. I have learned that the only way to overcome them is to stand up to them. When *they* know that *you* know that their bark is worse than their bite, any advantage they had over you disappears. It is not that difficult to beat a bully!

Our church cannot afford to be intimidated by the devil any longer. The world is dying without hope because, in too many cases, we have been afraid to tell them the truth. This will change when we decide to stop listening to culture and begin to use our voices to proclaim, with love, the full Gospel of our Lord. As firebrands in the pulpit and firebrands in the pew—men and women passionate about truth that sets people free—we can no longer watch in silence. It is time to speak up!

"For I am not ashamed of the gospel of Christ, for it is the power of God to salvation for everyone who believes, for the Jew first and also for the Greek. For in it the righteousness of God is revealed..." (Romans 1:16, 17 NKJV)

"But sanctify the Lord God in your hearts, and always be ready to give a defense to everyone who asks you a reason for the hope that is in you, with meekness and fear." (I Peter 3:16 NKJV)

I truly feel the church has come to a crossroad. We have the choice of holding on and depending on our long established systems to sustain us, or we can lift our sails to the wind of the Spirit and allow Him to move us to a place of transformation and revival. I've got to tell you, I do not believe business as usual is a smart decision. I just believe we have been brought into the Kingdom for a time like this and God has big plans for His people. It is probably time to turn off some noise and tune in to the Spirit. He will reveal His will and plans to us if we will take time to listen.

Well...this is what I heard during my encounter with the Lord a few days ago. He is stirring me and calling me to move up. I feel it and I hear it. I am confident I am not the only one to whom He is speaking. As a matter of fact, I believe those heavenly radio waves are bouncing off your walls right now! Please don't miss what God is wanting to say and do in you. He wants to make His Word and will clear for you. Be a receiver, tune in to His frequency and let His voice resonate in your life.

God is speaking. Make sure you are listening.

AN EXERCISE IN CONTEMPLATION
Placing What I Just Read Into My Ministry Context

1. What are your takeaways from this chapter? How can it be applied to your life and ministry?

2. What is God saying to you when you pray? What is your response to what He is saying to you? How is your service to God being affected by what He is saying to you?

3. What are some things in your life that are keeping you from hearing from the Lord? What are you doing to overcome these obstacles?

PRAYER ASSIGNMENT

Thank the Lord for being a personal God who longs to have communion with you. Repent of the times you have allowed things to stand in your way, making communication with Him difficult. Open your heart to His voice and let Him know nothing is more important than receiving a clear word from Him. Let Him know you are ready to wake up, make up, show up and speak up—you genuinely want to be on the same frequency with Him. Give Him praise for all He is doing in your life and ministry.

CHAPTER 19

It's Going To Take Some Time

(Posted October 28, 2021)

I remember when the Internet first came to the Higgins home. We were all so excited to think the world would be available at our fingertips. We would be able to get information and learn about anything that interested us. We could not wait for this new opportunity to explore and grow. This happened for us in the mid '90s.

I still remember sitting down at the computer—after Donna or Kris showed me how to turn it on—and hearing that awful sound as connection was being made. And, oh, that spinning circle—that thing drove me crazy! It seemed to take forever before anything could be done, and I have to tell you, I lost interest pretty quickly! It did not take me long until I realized everything I needed to know was in a book somewhere—I would leave this innovative technology to others.

I must admit I have come around to a greater appreciation of the Internet these days, but I still get frustrated when I hit a glitch or the speed is not up to par. I do not like to wait. If I want it, I would like to have it now. Patience may be a virtue but there is still quite a bit of room for growth in this area of my life! I get the feeling almost every day I am not alone in this!

Unfortunately, this desire for the quick and convenient has reached into most areas of our personal world. The most important things to most of us are the clock and the next thing on our schedule. It is getting harder and harder to enjoy the journey because our focus is, too often, only on the destination. Our rush and insistence on the instant are causing us to miss so much.

I would like to think this problem has not invaded the church and affected us spiritually, but it has. Old fashioned ideas of tarrying and waiting on the Lord are rarely discussed. Process is a bad word. Discipleship is a word used but not understood.

LEADERSHIP THOUGHTS

We know the things of God are important but they have a lot of competition in our lives. Prayer, worship, and the Word are all necessary, but they must fit into our schedule. This is the sad commentary of our day.

Something must change! We all know this is true, however, we spend more time pontificating about the problem than we do trying to change it. It is as though we have accepted the current situation as the new norm and simply say, "It is what it is." But, if I understand properly, one responsibility of the church is to confront culture, not comply with it. We are to be different, set the bar high and demonstrate to the world a better way. Blending is not our goal but reflecting Jesus and leading people to Him is.

While I am not trying to create a Pollyanna world, I think revisiting some things in our history may be helpful. Not everything from yesterday needs to be discarded. By searching through the archives of the past we may discover some direction that will lead us to a healthier and happier place. Pulling up some memories and drawing from some experiences may be just what is needed for these times.

When I think about my formative years as a believer, one thing stands out that I am convinced made a huge difference in my development—the altar. The altar was more than a piece of furniture in our church; it was the place where people connected with God. If you could find those altars that were in the Norman Oklahoma, Classen Boulevard Church of God in the late '70s, I'm sure you could find some tear stains left there by a searching college student who just wanted to find God's will for his life. It was here I poured out my heart to God and had encounters with Him that continue to impact my life today. Those experiences changed me, shaped me, and set me on a path to my destiny.

In our church, we always had times of personal ministry where people would come forward to be anointed with oil and prayed for. But we seemed to understand the difference between personal ministry, where people came seeking a blessing, and altar time, where we humbled ourselves before God and experienced genuine intimacy with Him. The blessings were needed but our time with the Father around the altar was life changing.

It was at the altar where I learned the importance of tarrying before the Lord. The word tarry means to linger in expectation or to wait. You cannot rush tarrying. You cannot predict how long you will need to tarry. Tarrying requires a willingness to wait until…until you pray through—until the burden is lifted—until you are certain the answer is on the way. Tarrying is going to take some time.

It was while we tarried before the Lord that revelation came; development and growth took place and genuine spiritual depth was gained. It was while we tarried our flesh was crucified and a true life in the Spirit became possible. It was while we tarried conviction came to the house and people were drawn to the Lord. It required great discipline, but the results were absolutely worth it.

I realize changing times effect the way ministry is done today. Whereas we have learned to do some things better and great progress has been made on many fronts, there is still the realization that a revival in our church and an awakening in our world is needed. We do thank God for our blessings and celebrate our many victories…but deep in our hearts we know more is needed. We cannot deny the fact that many churches are in decline and many pastors are frustrated. We certainly cannot deny the fact that our world is in trouble and shows no sign of improving.

The great challenge will be to cast off expectations that have been placed upon us and look steadfastly to the Lord for direction. Our decisions cannot be driven by numbers. A weekend revival will not be enough. A new sermon series may produce some fruit, but it will probably not bring in the harvest. Do not be shocked when business as usual generates only the usual business. There has to be more!

More...that is what we need. More...that is God's plan. More... it can happen where you live and serve. It can, but...it calls for a God encounter. This will always happen at the altar when you wait...when you tarry. You want it suddenly but suddenly is usually preceded by waiting. This may not be what you want to hear but the old adage, "good things come to those who wait," is true! God has a good plan for your life and ministry but—get ready—it is going to take some time.

"But those who wait on the Lord shall renew their strength; They shall mount up with wings like eagles, They shall run and not be weary, They shall walk and not faint." (Isaiah 40:31 NKJV)

AN EXERCISE IN CONTEMPLATION
Placing What I Just Read Into My Ministry Context

1. What are your takeaways from this chapter? How can it be applied to your life and ministry?

2. How long has it been since you truly tarried before the Lord in prayer? What was the result of waiting on the Lord? Was the result worth the sacrifice you made to tarry?

3. Think about the statement, "Do not be shocked when business as usual generates only the usual business." How can this be applied to your ministry? What do you feel the Lord is wanting to do differently in you to increase your fruitfulness? Are you willing to make the change?

> **PRAYER ASSIGNMENT**
>
> Find a quiet place to simply spend time in the Lord's presence. Love Him, thank Him and praise Him—do not rush. Talk to Him just like you would talk to your best friend. Listen carefully as He speaks to you. Let this time change you as you tarry before Him. Let a pattern begin with this experience that carries over to other encounters with the Father. Learn the blessing of waiting on the Lord.

CHAPTER 20

The Call To Swim Upstream

(Posted January 16, 2022)

One of the most fascinating occurrences in nature, of which I have read, is the migration of salmon. This fish is born in freshwater rivers, spends most of its life in saltwater but returns to the river of its birth for spawning. The challenge of this process is, in order to reach its destination, it must swim upstream; it must swim against the river's current.

This is no easy feat for the salmon. There are many obstacles such as rapids and debris in the path. There are predators such as bears and sport fishermen intent on catching them. The journey, itself, may be a few hundred miles in length. All these challenges fight against the process, yet the determined salmon assume this task every fall.

I have been thinking a lot about swimming upstream; moving against the tide. I have come to the conclusion this is not just behavior for the salmon, but it must become the lifestyle of the believer. I understand the Christian walk has always been in opposition to the world, but today's climate takes it to a whole new level. The words of Paul to the Romans have never been more important—*"And do not be conformed to this world, but be transformed by the renewing of your mind, that you may prove what is that good and acceptable and perfect will of God." (Romans 12:2 NKJV)*

The environment in which we find ourselves has become so corrupt and perverted. The prophet, Isaiah, said there would come a time when men would *"call evil good and good evil" (Isaiah 5:20 NKJV)*. Paul told Timothy in the latter times, *"Some will depart from the faith, giving heed to deceiving spirits and doctrines of devils, speaking lies in hypocrisy, having their own conscience seared with a hot iron" (I Timothy 4:1-2 NKJV)*. These two prophetic statements have become reality in our present culture. We do, indeed, live in perilous and evil days.

The challenge for the church is how will we respond to these times. It is an absolute fact, everything we do must be rooted in love. It is also true that we must not be afraid to adjust and modernize our methods in order to experience our maximum effectiveness. But...while we intentionally reach out to the world in love and use every means available to us to communicate the message, we must not fail to speak truth. It is only when people know the truth that they will be set free. (John 8:32)

The old adage, "it is easier said than done," certainly comes into play here. It is not easy—in fact, it is quite difficult—to stand against the crowd and boldly declare what the Holy Scriptures say. It will never be popular to take a position against sin and the intimidation from the secular culture will be strong against those who do. Media, entertainment, and perceived public opinion have drawn a line in the sand on the side of anti-Biblical lifestyles and behavior, accusing those who oppose these to be narrow minded, bigoted and hatemongers. The challenge is real.

To further complicate matters, many church leaders and members have chosen popularity and self-preservation over standing for Biblical truth. To avoid offending anyone, an attitude of "go along to get along" has become the unspoken strategy. Condoning sin is not the plan but avoiding the subject is. Neutrality has become their position of choice.

But...even with an awareness of the lay of the land, I seem to be hearing the Lord say, "I'm looking for some people to swim upstream!" The call is going out for men and women to live holy lives in an unholy world and proclaim liberating truth to those bound by the lies of the devil. The call is not to mean people or self-righteous people but to broken people—people with tear dimmed eyes—people moved by compassion. The call is for people who realize this life is temporary, but eternity is forever. Our Lord is calling...

This subject is stirring in my spirit. I have been dreaming about it at night and meditating upon it during the day. I believe God is calling me—not to the familiar—but to something fresh and more productive than I have ever experienced. This "new thing" God is wanting to do is going to require I leave my comfort zone and surrender to the call to swim upstream. Some who have been with me may not go with me on this new journey. Some things I have used in the past may need to be left behind this time. Some things that have been important may not be now. Whatever sacrifice or change is required, I must be willing to assume them.

A couple of nights ago, I woke up from a dream with the following outline clearly in my spirit. I quickly wrote it down because I felt it was instruction for my journey upstream. I believe this is what the Lord said to me:

STAY ENCOURAGED

Events and situations around me may naturally cause discouragement. It is during these times I must take personal responsibility for my attitude and outlook. I Samuel 30:6 says, "David encouraged himself in the Lord his God." David's approach to his situation must be mine as well.

It has never been more important for me to stay in the Word and constantly practice walking in the Spirit. His Word and presence will be my source of courage. No one can keep me from this but me! It is my responsibility to stay encouraged.

TRAVEL LIGHT

Sometimes I carry things that only serve to weigh me down. Some things, to which I have become attached, serve no useful purpose in my mission—they take my time and energy but do not really help me on my journey. It is probably time for some housecleaning and decluttering.

This is surely what the writer to the Hebrews was conveying when he said, *"...Let us lay aside every weight, and the sin which so easily ensnares us, and let us run with endurance the race that is set before us."* (Hebrews 12:1) I do not want to carry anything that hinders my progress.

DO NOT BE AFRAID

Fear is torment. Fear is paralyzing. Fear is an enemy of faith. Fear has a strong grip and, if allowed to take root in us, will destroy us.

The devil is throwing the kitchen sink at us, today, as it relates to fear. We are afraid of a virus. We are afraid of rising crime rates. We are afraid of an economy going the wrong direction. We are afraid for our children's future. We are afraid for our own future. The list goes on and on.

The disciples learned the answer to the fear issue when they accompanied Jesus to the Mount of Transfiguration. The events of that occasion caused them to fall down in fear. At that moment, *"Jesus came and touched them and said, "Arise, and do not be afraid." When they had lifted up their eyes, they saw no one but Jesus only"* (Matthew 17:7-8 NKJV). They discovered when they looked to Jesus, they saw nothing to be afraid of. I do not want to forget this simple lesson.

GET READY FOR ADVENTURE

I think it is interesting that the word "adventure" was in my dream. An adventure is an exciting experience or undertaking that is typically bold and sometimes risky. I am convinced this is exactly where God is calling us—to a place of bold moves that may appear risky to our flesh and friends, but totally align with God's will for our lives. Many in former generations have stood while the masses bowed—it may now be our turn to take a stand.

We have been praying—we need to keep praying. We have been strategizing—there is nothing wrong with having a plan. We have been dreaming—most things begin with a dream. But, at some point, we have to leave the shore and step into the water. A stand has to be taken. A side has to be chosen.

Some will not understand, and others will adamantly oppose, but if the Word says it, we will obey. We will hold to our convictions and seek to please the Lord in all we do. We are not seeking affirmation or promotion—we just want to be participants in what God has planned for these last days...even if it means swimming upstream!

LEADERSHIP THOUGHTS

AN EXERCISE IN CONTEMPLATION
Placing What I Just Read Into My Ministry Context

1. What are your takeaways from this chapter? How can it be applied to your life and ministry?

2. How do you, personally, interpret the admonition in Scripture to "be not conformed to this world"? How difficult is it for you to be different from the world? Are there areas in your Christian walk that need improvement with this?

3. What is God calling you to that will require you to swim upstream? Are you willing to do this? What will be the consequences of your disobedience? What will be the results of your obedience?

PRAYER ASSIGNMENT

Ask God for boldness and courage to stand for Him in this evil time. Be willing for Him to convict you of areas of your life that are more in line with the world than with His Word. Seek His transforming power in your daily walk, allowing you to represent Him in a way that pleases Him and points others to Him. Give Him praise for calling you into the Kingdom and using you as a witness to the world around you.

CHAPTER 21

Making Healing Front And Center

(Posted February 17, 2022)

MAKING HEALING FRONT AND CENTER

The ministry of Jesus was multi-faceted, to say the least. He touched every area of society and truly made an impact everywhere he went. But it seems, whatever the occasion, He was always healing the sick. Healing sick people was a priority of our Lord. *"Then Jesus went about all the cities and villages, teaching in their synagogues, preaching the gospel of the kingdom, and healing every sickness and every disease among the people."* (Matthew 9:35)

Healing has been one of the most misused and misunderstood doctrines of the Bible for as long as I remember. From the total deniers, who say healing is not available today, to the "I am healed and can never be sick" crowd, so many have missed the mark and led people to false doctrine. It seems this is a classic example of what the devil likes to do to keep us from liberating truth.

I grew up in an environment where the subject of healing was commonplace. I have often said, it seemed every Sunday night in the church I attended—at some point in every service—healing would be mentioned. We prayed for the sick. We sent anointed prayer cloths to the sick folks who could not be in the service. The message of healing was front and center in everything we did.

Unfortunately, we have arrived at a time when healing has been deemphasized by many. While some churches still preach and practice praying for the sick, others never bring up the subject. A large segment of the population who attend church every week have no idea about the 39 stripes brutally placed on the back of our Lord before His crucifixion, allowing us to claim I Peter 2:24, *"...by whose stripes you were healed."* This is information that does not need to be ignored—it needs to be shouted from the rooftops!

In my spirit, I hear the Lord saying, now is the time to take the message of divine healing from the back of the paper and return it to the front page. I believe as the church begins to make its way out of our present time of reset, a mighty move of the Spirit is in our near future. It just keeps coming to me over and over, this season of revival will be a time of multiplied miracles. I fully expect the power of God to be manifested among us in ways unprecedented in our lifetime. I really believe this!

But as we enter this fresh season of New Testament power, I believe there are two things that must be clearly understood and taught: 1) God heals for His glory and 2) Our God is absolutely sovereign.

GOD HEALS FOR HIS GLORY

God is not interested in making us famous—whereas our testimony is important, He will not allow our star to be brighter than His. This may sound harsh, but His emphasis is not even on making the sick well. Everything He does is for His Kingdom and He wants all the glory. Our attitude must be that of John the Baptist—we must decrease so that He might increase. (John 3:30) We will see a huge upsurge in healing when the attention leaves the one praying and the one being prayed for, and goes completely to God.

OUR GOD IS ABSOLUTELY SOVEREIGN

This means God has the absolute right to do all things according to His own good pleasure. While we pray about what is happening now, God answers with eternity in mind. He works with the big picture—not just what we see and feel in the present. Praying in faith is not just believing we will have our prayer answered, it is putting the issue totally in the hands of God for Him to do what is best for us and the Kingdom. This is not a tool to help us save face for when we pray for healing and it does not come; it is putting our complete trust in a good

God. Like Job, we are able to say, *"Though He slay me, yet will I trust Him." (Job 3:15)*

When we accept these two basic tenets of faith, we can go boldly to the throne of God and pray for healing. We can trust the hand and heart of God knowing He loves us and has a good plan for us. We can believe this even when the outward evidence does not speak of physical healing, for sometimes God's plan is a glorified body and not a healed physical body. It is at this time, we stand firmly on II Corinthians 4:16-18, *"Therefore we do not lose heart. Even though our outward man is perishing, yet the inward man is being renewed day by day. For our light affliction, which is but for a moment, is working for us a far more exceeding and eternal weight of glory, while we do not look at the things which are seen, but at the things which are not seen..."*

The healing, to which I just referred, was purchased for us on the cross. Jesus died so eternal life could be experienced by those who believe on Him. This life lived in the eternal realm is beautiful with no sickness or suffering of any kind. People who die in the faith, absolutely lay down a body that may have been ravaged by disease, and take on one that will never feel another pain. This is the ultimate healing with which all believers will be rewarded one day.

But, please hear me, death is not the only means to healing. When Jesus died on the cross, He paid the price for eternal life, which entitles us to live with Him forever in a glorified body. If there was nothing more, it seems to me the scourging (whipping) He took before He got to the cross was not necessary. But it was necessary! For at the whipping post—with leather straps embedded with bone and lead lashed across his back—He bought divine healing for us! Thirty-nine hateful and excruciating stripes were placed on His back so that we would be healed.

Healing must be particularly important to our Lord if He was willing to endure such intense and agonizing pain to pay for it. Since He went through immense torture for healing to be available to His children, He must want us to have it. I can only conclude, it is my right as a child of God to pray for healing and believe Him to do it. I can know Him as the Savior of my soul and the healer of my body.

Most people in my circle will agree, healing is scriptural and obtainable but simply believing in it is not enough. We must capture, again, the once prevalent passion for the full Gospel which includes divine healing. We cannot allow ourselves to be intimidated by the devil or marginalized by our society. We cannot allow the excesses of charlatans and the misuses of spiritual gifts to keep us from receiving this much needed blessing our Lord suffered to provide for us. We must allow the healing rivers of the Holy Spirit to, again, flow through us. I am convinced this is the will of God.

As stated earlier in this blog, I deeply believe supernatural revival is on the way. This revival will be marked by multitudes of people from all over the globe coming into the Kingdom. Many of these will be drawn to the Lord by verified testimonies of divine healing. Just as in the New Testament, God will use the display of His power to get the attention of people. There is just no good reason this mighty move of the Spirit should miss your church!

So, what do we do? Pray for the sick. Preach and teach divine healing. Believe for miracles. Stand squarely on the Word of God—nothing more, nothing less—and watch the Father do for you what He promised. And...through it all, give Him all the glory!

"Is anyone among you sick? Let him call for the elders of the church, and let them pray over him, anointing him with oil in the name of the Lord. And the prayer of faith will save the sick, and the Lord will raise Him up. And if he has committed sins, he will be forgiven." (James 5:14-15)

Healing has been provided for you in the atoning blood of the Lord, Jesus. This beautiful gift is part of your spiritual inheritance. Receive it today. Be healed in the name of Jesus.

LEADERSHIP THOUGHTS

AN EXERCISE IN CONTEMPLATION
Placing What I Just Read Into My Ministry Context

1. What are your takeaways from this chapter? How can it be applied to your life and ministry?

2. What are some testimonies you have, or have heard, of divine healing? How do these testimonies encourage you to pray and believe for healing in your body and in the bodies of people you know and love? Are you expecting healing to occur?

3. What is your reaction when you pray for healing, but it does not come? Does this affect your willingness to continue praying for healing? Are you truly willing to trust a sovereign God to answer according to His plan?

> **PRAYER ASSIGNMENT**
>
> Remind yourself of healings in the Word of God and testimonies of which you are personally aware. Let these examples build your faith as you take needs of healing to the Lord in prayer. Be bold in your prayer as you bring specific needs to Him. Let praise and thanksgiving overflow in your spirit as you believe God for divine healing in your body and in others.

CHAPTER 22

The Blessing Of Barrenness

(Posted March 26, 2022)

Many old western movies have begun with that scene of a deserted town with the wind blowing a tumbleweed down what, at one time, had been a bustling street. Or, there is the scene of a dusty field with the remnants of a crop still there, but now it is mostly dry, parched soil with no sign of life to be found. Of course, we have all seen the one of the scorching sun beaming down in the desert, as the camera slowly moves to reveal the bones of the cowboy that did not survive. The one thing each of these movie scenes have in common is barrenness.

Barren is a truly harsh word. It actually means, bleak and lifeless. Other words sometimes used to describe it are unproductive, infertile, unfruitful, desert; desolate, waste, impoverished...nothing good is found in this list! I even decided to ask Google what a barren life is—the answer was, "You achieve no success in it." It seems to me that this is one thing everyone should, by all means, avoid!

But despite information provided by search engines or images depicted in movies, seasons of barrenness are not always bad. In fact, there are countless examples of bleak times being the turning point to some of life's greatest victories.

Moses is forced to flee from his royal life in Egypt to tend his father-in-law's sheep on the backside of the desert. It sure looks like he fell fast and hard, but in Exodus 3, he has an encounter with God through a burning bush that not only changed his life, but changed a nation.

Hannah lived a life of sorrow and humiliation because, according to I Samuel 1:5, *"the Lord has shut up her womb."* Her adversary constantly ridiculed Hannah because of this condition. But God had a plan—at just the right time she became pregnant and gave birth to a son. At a moment in history when the nation had become spiritually bankrupt and leaderless, God used Hannah's son, Samuel, to be a mighty prophet in Israel.

Paul had been one of the most ardent fighters against the Cross but, after his conversion, used all that he had to fight for the Christ of Calvary. This strong commitment to Jesus led him to be hated by the Jews and imprisoned. His living conditions were, many times, harsh and, no doubt, he felt forsaken. But instead of using this desolate time as an opportunity for self-pity, Paul wrote what are referred to as his prison epistles—Ephesians, Philippians, Colossians, and Philemon.

John was banished to the Isle of Patmos *"for the word of God and the testimony of Jesus Christ."(Revelation 1:9)* I would imagine those responsible for sending him to this deserted place felt they were getting rid of him, but little did they know they were positioning him for a divine encounter with Jesus! It was during this time of isolation the last book of the New Testament was written.

I must admit, my personal desire is to stay as far removed from barrenness as possible. One of my greatest joys is to look back at the end of a day and see productivity and gain. I want to think my life counts and my work matters. The thought of an unproductive life causes indescribable sorrow and disappointment. But...I have to say, sometimes seasons of barrenness come. From time to time, I find myself in the desert—nothing is working—alone even in a crowd—confused with no direction—wondering if my best days are behind me. Perhaps that is too transparent, but it is the truth. It has happened to me, and probably, if you are honest, it has happened to you.

But, if we genuinely believe God is at work in our lives, always for our good, then we must know there are blessings even in barrenness! Your prison cell or deserted island can become your place of miraculous provision and revelation. His plan for your life does not stop during the barren season; this season could even be part of the plan.

You may ask, what possible blessing can there be in barrenness? I do not pretend to have all the answers, but I know from experience, there are at least three things that happen when I find myself in the desert.

GOD SPEAKS

The four examples from the Bible I mentioned earlier in the blog have something in common—they all found themselves in a barren place. Read their stories, however, and you will discover they had something else in common—God spoke to them in their barrenness.

I am convinced the hardest time to hear from God is when we are moving forward with momentum. Our tendency is to give ourselves to the moment and ride the wave—what we are doing is working, so we relax and enjoy it. God has something to say to us even in these moments but, many times, our spiritual antennae is not operating at full frequency. But in the valley… in that hard, lonely place…we become desperate, causing our heart to cry out to God.

God—as the good Father He is—will reveal himself when we cry out to Him in our desperation. He says things we need to hear. He gives revelation we could not receive any other time. He teaches truth that will literally change our lives. He does His best work in us when the distractions of success and the busyness of life have subsided. He has our attention, and He takes advantage of it.

I HAVE A GREAT OPPORTUNITY TO FULLY ALIGN WITH HIS PLAN

It is so easy to get out of alignment. This happens with my vehicle, occasionally, and can cause real damage if it is not corrected. The problem is, it occurs so slightly over time—I can miss it if I am not paying attention.

In ministry—in life—it is easy to get out of alignment with God's plan. We commit to systems. We listen to the advice of others. We follow trends. Often, in our effort to do good, we try to do things we are not called to do and be things we are not called to be. Even in sincerity and purity, we can become misaligned if we are not careful.

In my season of barrenness, God speaks, and if I am smart, I listen. He will show me what needs to come off and what needs to be put on. He will reaffirm His call on my life and give opportunity for fresh commitment to it. He will use this experience to shape and prepare me for my next assignment. This dormant time in my life is not wasted—it is my chance to fully align with His plan.

OTHERS ARE AFFECTED

God's plan for me in my barren season is not to simply make me feel better but to change me! His desire is never short-sighted but always far reaching. His intention is to take me to a higher level and use me in ways I have never even imagined. His blessing on my life is to make my life a blessing to others. What happens to me will affect someone else.

The people who saw me exiled to Patmos will hear my revelation. Those who mourned my imprisonment will benefit from my accomplishments there. Those who ridiculed my barrenness will have to acknowledge my blessing. Those who wondered where I have gone will witness my return. These are things my earlier examples could have said, I will have my own testimony when this trying time comes to an end! My story will affect others and God will get the glory!

As I am writing this blog, I am sensing there will be those reading it who are experiencing a season of barrenness. You do not understand why things have happened as they have—it really makes no sense. Perhaps your ministry…or your marriage…or your career…or something else important to you has taken a turn you did not anticipate. If you could explain it and figure out the why, it would be so much easier to handle…but you cannot. You are on an island…it is lonely and deserted…the reality of barrenness is staring you in the face.

You can throw in the towel and quit…a lot of others have done this. You can become bitter and play the part of a victim… that is a common response today. You can feel sorry for yourself and drown in a pool of self-pity…some would even say you are justified to do this. You can do any of these things, knowing you will not be the first to take whatever route you choose to take.

I am hoping, however, you will have a different reaction to your situation. Even in your pain and confusion, I am hoping you will start looking for the heart and hand of the Father. I boldly declare to you, God still has a plan for your life…He is not finished with you…He will make you fruitful and productive again!

Bishop Tim Hill, Presiding Bishop of the Church of God, wrote a song several years ago that speaks directly to those needing the message of this blog. With his permission, I share the chorus of, "It Will Rain Again"—

But it will rain again,
The fruit will fill the vine.
The stalk will bend with wheat;
The grapes burst forth with wine.
So go into the field,

Your work is not in vain.

God promised harvest and I know it will rain.

Get up, my friend. It is about to rain, again, on your dry, parched heart. Even with everything going on your life you are about to discover there is a blessing in your barrenness.

AN EXERCISE IN CONTEMPLATION
Placing What I Just Read Into My Ministry Context

1. What are your takeaways from this chapter? How can it be applied to your life and ministry?

2. Have you ever experienced a barren season in your life? Were there lessons you learned during this time? How has your life and ministry been impacted by barrenness?

3. How are you using your season of barrenness to help others and advance the Kingdom? What has been the effect of your story? How do you plan to continue using your testimony to be a blessing?

PRAYER ASSIGNMENT:

Resist the natural inclination to complain about your barren season and ask God to help you see what He wants you to see during this time. Pray for Him to help you remain faithful and fully surrender your all to Him. Instead of this being a time of defeat, claim this as a defining moment in your spiritual development. Give God praise for the marvelous work He is doing in your life and ministry right now.

CHAPTER 23
Rising To The Challenge
(Posted July 12, 2022)

By necessity, every level of leadership in any organization, including the church, must give diligent attention to methods and management. Systems are developed to allow these to be delivered and appropriated in every situation. These systems are there to provide order and create a path that moves the organization along in a prescribed manner. We call it administration. It's a good idea and even one ordained in Scripture.

Successful organizations will always be supported by pillars of absolutes. These are non-negotiable tenets. They are set in stone. Everyone in the organization knows what they are and has a firm commitment to them. These absolutes establish the very reason for the life of the organization.

Along with the absolutes will be other moving parts allowing the organization to adjust to situations and events. These moving parts are the systems mentioned in the first paragraph of this article. They can be adjusted and modified to accommodate the present need. They are not set in stone. They should always be seen as tools.

When you understand that an organization must be grounded by absolutes, supported by systems, you can say that organization must be steadfast, yet flexible. It must be firmly established on a solid foundation while agile enough to adapt to the changing climate it is called to address. It must be entrenched in its purpose but not in its methods.

These facts cannot be ignored by the church of the 21st century. We have to be careful to remain true to the foundational absolutes upon which we have been built. We must also continually hone the delivery systems necessary to keep us effective in these constantly changing times.

What are the absolutes for the church? Some may put together a long list, but I believe they could all be combined into two areas—the Word of God and, what I like to call, the love mandate.

THE WORD OF GOD

When time is no more, the Word of God will still be. It is God-breathed and infallible. It has stood the test of time and remains as relevant today as when it was written. It is the litmus test for all questions and disputes. Nothing man says or does can supersede it. Church doctrine and practice must begin and end with the Word. It is THE absolute for the church.

THE LOVE MANDATE

The purpose and mission of everything the church is and does must be driven by one thing—love. Our time with God in prayer and worship is inspired by love. Our service is motivated by what motved Him—love. The words of our Lord, Himself, capture the importance and priority of love:

"And you shall love the Lord your God with all your heart, with all your soul, with all your mind, and with all your strength. This is the first commandment. And the second, like it, is this: You shall love your neighbor as yourself. There is no other commandment greater than these." (Mark 12:30-31)

These foundational principles cannot be considered optional or elective. They are not affected by culture or opinion. They are always absolute for every church, everywhere.

The great challenge for the contemporary church is ensuring its systems are adequate to deliver the message and keep it in a position for mass effectiveness. The assumption that our methods of operation do not need adjustment is the assumption that was made by many formerly successful, yet now non-existent, businesses and churches. We must not die because of system failure.

Here are some facts to consider:

1. Absolutes are sacred; systems are not.
2. Absolutes are why we exist; systems are tools to accomplish the mission.
3. Healthy organizations will continually adjust/tweak/change systems.
4. There is great danger when we choose to worship at the altar of our systems.

The present challenges facing the church are no match for our message. As a matter of fact, our message is the answer to these challenges! Now, as never before, the world needs to hear what we have been preaching for years—there is hope and help in Jesus! He will bring us through this storm victoriously!

The present challenges, however, are testing our systems. Our delivery methods are under attack. If we ignore this and assume that, once the storm subsides, we will return to business as usual, we could find ourselves in a very bad place. But if we are willing to be placed on God's potter's wheel and submit to a time of remolding and retooling, we can be positioned for greatness. Instead of this being the beginning of the end, it can be the beginning of our best days!

The following questions need to be asked by any church desiring to have a place and be strong in these times:

1. What has God called your church to be and do?
2. Do your present methods/structure place you in a position to accomplish this?
3. If not, what needs to happen for you to align with His plan?

The tasks may feel daunting but God will help us. I am encouraged by something that happened to Nehemiah when he found himself in need of the Lord's help. Nehemiah 7:5 (MEV) says, *"So my God put an idea in my mind..."* I believe, if we will pray and listen, God will speak. He will instruct and lead us to fresh and innovative methods that will glorify Him and increase our harvest.

I am not blind to the obstacles we face—they are real and must not be ignored. At the same time, I am confidently mindful of the promise of Jesus that the gates of Hell would not prevail against His church. I'm not giving up; I will rise to the challenge by adjusting my sail and move in the direction the wind of the Spirit is blowing. I'm thankful for my past but it pales in comparison to where He is leading me. I really believe, this is our time and the best is yet to come!

AN EXERCISE IN CONTEMPLATION
Placing What I Just Read Into My Ministry Context

1. What are your takeaways from this chapter? How can it be applied to your life and ministry?

2. What are the foundational absolutes in your ministry for which you are committed? Are there adequate systems in place to ensure you are able to operate at your maximum effectiveness? What could you do to make your ministry even more effective?

3. What are some challenges you face in the operation of your ministry? How are these challenges being addressed? Are you praying for creative ideas to overcome your challenges and advance the ministry?

> **PRAYER ASSIGNMENT**
>
> Be willing to make a fresh commitment to the call of God and the ministry to which you have been assigned. Do not hesitate to bring your challenges to the Lord but do so with the confidence He is helping you and has called you to triumph. Boldly ask God for creative ideas to make you more effective and in alignment with His plan. Praise Him for victory.

CHAPTER 24

When God Is Silent

(Posted August 6, 2022)

Growing up in a very traditional Pentecostal church, one of my favorite parts of our worship service was testimony time. This was the time when anyone and everyone was given the opportunity to speak and share with the congregation what God had done for them. Some would stand out of peer pressure or obligation and repeat memorized lines—I was usually one of those. Some saw this as an opportunity to preach a little and seemed to enjoy the momentary spotlight. But the ones that truly moved me were those who reported accounts of recently answered prayer. These testimonies of God's intervention lifted everyone's faith and brought great encouragement.

So many songs we sang in my church were about God always hearing and answering prayer. The sermons I heard and the lessons I was taught told me God was involved in my life and He orchestrated all my affairs. I remember hearing people talk about God leading them and speaking to them. I came to believe in a very personal God who was active in my life.

These foundational truths taught to me as a child remain a bedrock in my life today. I have many personal examples of God moving and His voice directing me through some rough and rocky terrain. But, as Paul Harvey would say, I need to relay the rest of the story—it hasn't always happened for me just like the songs and sermons seemed to say. There have been times in my life I have cried out to God but... He was silent.

Sometimes God is silent—wow! How in the world can this be true? We know He is the loving Father who watches over us and is concerned about everything that concerns us. We know His presence is constant and nothing can separate us from His love. We know He feels our pain and is moved by our afflictions. But sometimes when we pray, He is silent.

This is a hard fact for many in the modern church to grasp—especially the modern American church. We have heard over and over we can have whatever we confess. A portrayal of God has emerged that more closely resembles a mythical genie in a bottle than the eternal Father exalted on His throne. Many have embraced a misleading narrative that depicts a God who serves us, rather than emphasizing our duty to serve Him. No wonder we are frustrated and confused when answers to prayer do not come.

This would probably be a good time for all of us to stop for a moment and reconsider roles—He is the creator; we are the created. We should probably also consider perspective—we see with very limited vision; He sees the big picture. We should probably not forget time and space—we think in terms of now; He operates with eternity in mind. Quite simply—He is God; we are not. He is perfect in all His ways—even when He does not speak to our requests.

So what should our response be to those times when He is silent?

CLING TO WHAT WE KNOW

Some things are true no matter what. Circumstances cannot change them and time only makes them more real. These are facts that will not change—God is good, God loves us, and God is with us. In the most difficult of situations, grabbing hold of what we know and refusing to let go will be the basis of our sustained victory. There is nothing the devil can do to overcome us if we doggedly cling to what we know.

PRACTICE HIS PRESENCE

The people with whom you are most comfortable are those with whom you can spend the most time without talking. You are close enough to them, you can actually enjoy simply being in their company. There will never be many of these people in your life but when you have one, they are special indeed.

A true mark of spiritual maturity is learning to enjoy the Lord—not just being happy for what He does for us but savoring every moment in His presence. Joy and peace abound when we begin to hunger more for Him than we do His blessings. Being fulfilled by His presence should be the goal of every child of God.

EXPECT THE BENEFITS OF WAITING.

Most people do not like to wait. Our culture is one that moves fast and wants what it wants now. A friend of mine told me, one time he looked for the express lane at the car wash! Patience is not a valued virtue today.

But, here is a fact worth remembering—God is not moved by culture. He places tremendous value on waiting. As a matter of fact, He does His best work in us between the asking and receiving. It is in that in-between time he molds and perfects us. Business really picks up in our life when we start looking for the benefits of waiting on the Lord.

"But those who wait on the Lord shall renew their strength; They shall mount up with wings like eagles, They shall run and not be weary, They shall walk and not faint." (Isaiah 40:31 NKJV)

KNOW HE HAS A PLAN

God is many wonderful things in my life, but the one thing in which I may be the most grateful is the fact He is my Father. He really loves me as His child and, as a good Father, He wants what is best for me. He has a plan for my life and everything He does for me has that plan clearly in mind—even when I do not see it or understand it. I am comforted by this knowledge. I know I can trust His plan.

So, sometimes God is silent. That doesn't mean He did not hear. It certainly doesn't mean He doesn't care. The truth is, He always hears and He cares more than we can comprehend. Those sermons and songs I heard as a child, about Him always answering prayer, were not an exaggeration at all—He does always answer. He just answers when it is time, in the way that is best and in a manner for His glory.

My friend, do not be discouraged by God's silence. Let this experience work for your good. It is going to make you better. It is going to make you stronger. His silence is a sure sign that He is at work on your behalf. The silence of the Lamb of God will soon be replaced by the roar of the Lion of Judah. Get ready! He may be silent today but He will not be silent forever.

AN EXERCISE IN CONTEMPLATION
Placing What I Just Read Into My Ministry Context

1. What are your takeaways from this chapter? How can it be applied to your life and ministry?

2. Are there prayers you are praying that have not, yet, been answered? What is your response during this time of waiting? What lessons are you learning during this time of waiting?

3. Drawing from your own experience, how valuable have times been in your life when God was silent? How have these times shaped you and prepared you for what you are going through now?

PRAYER ASSIGNMENT

Recognize God as the mighty God He is—perfect in all His ways. Confess your commitment to Him regardless of what happens or does not happen in your life. Thank Him for the plan He has for you and verbalize your confidence in this plan coming to full fruition. Prepare your heart to receive all God has in His storehouse for you.

CHAPTER 25

God Is Calling—Will You Answer?

(Posted August 30, 2022)

Throughout history, pastors and other religious leaders have been at the forefront of significant societal change. Whether it was speaking out against injustice or speaking up for freedom, these men and women bravely placed themselves in peril to bring attention to issues that demanded action. They believed the cause was greater than their comfort and the price was one they were willing to pay.

The Church and those who lead within the church have always had far greater influence in what happens, or does not happen, in the world than many recognize. We see legislative bodies, politicians and those crowned by society as movers and shakers as the ones to credit, or blame, for life altering decisions. Whereas, these play a role on the big stage called life, they do not own the rights to the production. God is ultimately in control and His plan has always been to work through His Church and anointed leaders.

I have no doubt, my own life and worldview have been shaped by my experiences within the church and my association with its leaders. I still remember Sunday School teachers and lessons taught to me as a child. I recall sacred moments I spent with God around an altar of prayer, as I responded to an invitation given by my pastor. I am often reminded of truth—preached and taught to me by Godly servants of the Lord—that continues, to this day, to be a lamp to my feet and a light to my path.

As a young preacher trying to find my place and fulfill my calling, I will be forever grateful for mentors who invested time and energy in my life. These leaders spoke into my life, gave me opportunity for involvement and stood by me through my many mistakes. They were willing to correct me in love yet give me space to be who God was calling me to be. I have no doubt my blessings in ministry have come from God, but He delivered them to me through some incredibly special people.

God is still calling men and women to do His work in the earth. He will call some to stand before kings…He will call some to rally the masses…He will call some to eternally impact one… but answering the call, and being totally obedient to it, will be the single most important decision one will make after conversion.

You would be hard pressed, today, to find a greater need than that of holy, set apart men and women answering the call of God to be His voice, hands and heart to the world. These conveyors of truth are more than religious figures; they are instruments of the Lord to accomplish the mission He started when He came to this earth as a babe in a manger, more than two thousand years ago. The task given to these chosen vessels is from the Lord, and its fulfillment is necessary for the will of God to be done in the world.

"For whoever calls on the name of the Lord shall be saved. How then shall they call on Him in whom they have not believed? And how shall they believe in Him of whom they have not heard? And how shall they hear without a preacher? And how shall they preach unless they are sent? As it is written: How beautiful are the feet of those who preach the gospel of peace, Who bring glad tidings of good things!" (Romans 10:13-15 NKJV)

What an honor it is to be chosen by the Lord to do His work! But, over the years, I have watched how everyone responds to the call in different ways. From my viewpoint there are three levels of ministry commitment:

HEARD THE CALL

This person testifies to the call, perhaps is credentialed by an organization, and is content to occasionally share the Gospel. Without sounding too harsh—they simply include ministry in the many other involvements of their life. Ministry is not their priority.

FULFILLED BY THE CALL

This person identifies with the ministry. They are good at it. The ministry is their world—even their career. Advancement in rank and position is of utmost importance. They cannot imagine doing anything else.

DRIVEN BY THE CALL

This person may or may not be credentialed. They may or may not receive a paycheck to do it. They may or may not receive the recognition they deserve. But...they are passionate about the work of the Lord. They are never satisfied and are constantly looking for ways to do more. They are hungry for revival and burdened for the lost. Hearing the Father one day say, "well-done," is more important than accolades, positions, or titles. Pleasing God is all that matters.

I have to say, the person who simply has heard the call is going to make minimal impact, at best. The person who is fulfilled by the call will be tempted to operate in carnally (doing spiritual business in the flesh), and will find that much of his/her work will not stand the test of time. The person who is driven by the call will be anointed, productive and profitable in the Kingdom.

It is this "driven by the call" minister of the Gospel that God is using today. This one is developed in the prayer closet, refined in the fires of trial, and empowered by walking in the Spirit. Their spiritual eyes are open to needs around them and they refuse to look away. They will not be satisfied until all have heard and the mission has been completed.

I genuinely believe the windows of Heaven are open today—both to hear our prayers and respond with answers. The Holy

Spirit is anointing His servants to accomplish exploits and the fulfillment of His plan. But...I keep hearing Him say to me, "The open window is for a season." I believe He is saying, if I do not respond, He will move on to someone else. He is determined to complete His work—with or without me.

With or without me...what a sobering thought. My Pentecostal heritage will not be enough. My rank in ministry will not be enough. My expertise and giftings will not be enough. All that matters is my active commitment to the call of God.

All around us, the needs are many and the harvest is ripe. Never has there been greater opportunity to make an impact than today—real life-changing difference. The search is on and the call is going forth for vessels to be used in this end-time harvest. World changers are needed. You are eligible. "Here I am, send me" is all you have to say. When you do it, your world will never be the same.

AN EXERCISE IN CONTEMPLATION
Placing What I Just Read Into My Ministry Context

1. What are your takeaways from this chapter? How can it be applied to your life and ministry?

2. Of the three levels of ministry commitment—heard the call, fulfilled by the call, driven by the call—which one best describes your current commitment? Are you satisfied with where you are?

3. What are you doing to increase your ministry effectiveness? Is God pleased with your present standing?

PRAYER ASSIGNMENT

Understanding the call of God is both an honor and a responsibility, thank Him for calling you and ask Him to use you as He desires. Pray for a genuine burden that will keep you on task even when opposition is strong. Seek to be filled with the Holy Spirit enabling you to walk in the Spirit and accomplish remarkable things for the Kingdom. Praise Him, even in advance, for the breakthrough coming your way.

CHAPTER 26

This World Needs Us!

(Posted April 15, 2023)

THIS WORLD NEEDS US!

My favorite TV show of all time is the Andy Griffith Show. I have seen every episode countless times, but I still enjoy it and laugh at all the funny lines. There is nothing complicated about it—it's just good clean humor set in simpler times. I would much rather watch it than anything being produced by Hollywood today. I have often said, "Jesus, Andy and Barney have gotten me through a lot of hard places!"

One of the reasons I probably like the Andy Griffith Show is it reminds me of the small town in which I grew up. Hugo, Oklahoma in the '60s and '70s was "Mayberry-esque" to say the least. I think all the characters in the sitcom actually existed as real persons in my hometown! Family and friends were important to us. Things like morality, honesty and respect really mattered. God and the Church were at the forefront of all we did. I know things were not perfect, but looking back, they seemed pretty close.

When I compare where we are now in the world with where we were in my growing up years, I see two vastly different existences. Things are far more convenient now and the advancements of modern society, in so many ways, are mind-boggling. But...the depravity, lawlessness and disregard for God and His Word make this time extremely uncomfortable for me. I do not recognize my own country these days. I, quite frankly, don't feel at home here anymore.

Every now and then, I just get tired...tired of sin and ungodly lifestyles...tired of carnality and lukewarmness in the church... tired of the stress and strain of everyday living...tired of the suffering and pain of loved ones/friends...just plain tired! If I could hide from it, I would hide. If I could run away from it, I would run. If moving to a deserted island would be a true escape,

I would be willing to head that way at sunrise. Sometimes, I just get really tired.

Jesus surely knew these times would come when He prayed for us in John 17. He said to the Father, *"I have given them Your word; and the world has hated them because they are not of the world, just as I am not of the world. I do not pray that You should take them out of the world, but that You should keep them from the evil one."* (John 17:14-15) I hear Him saying, He knew we would face attack, hostility and hardship in this world. He did not pray we would be removed from these things, just kept safe in the Father's hand. He prayed this prayer, not only for His disciples, but for us, and it is a prayer for which we are seeing an answer every day!

When I read this beautiful prayer in John 17, it becomes crystal clear to me God has a plan for His children in this world, today. Jesus even said to the Father, *"As you sent Me into the world, I also have sent them into the world."* (John 17:18) When I am tired and tempted to run and hide, I am reminded I am part of God's plan. I cannot grow weary and give up. I must draw from His strength and fulfill my mission. God has called me, and this world needs me!

The realization that God has called me, and this world needs me, is sobering. I know me...my flaws...my weaknesses...my baggage. I do not feel I have that much to offer, and what I do have does not seem significant enough to make a difference. Yet, the One who knows me better than I know myself has chosen me to bear His name and represent Him in these chaotic times. This is His idea—His plan! *"You did not choose Me, but I chose you and appointed you that you should go and bear fruit, and that your fruit should remain, that whatever you ask the Father in my name, He may give you."* (John 15:16)

What could I possibly possess that the Father could use to impact this world? What contribution can I bring to the table that can make a difference? The answer is so simple, yet powerful when it is fully employed. It is not our talent, charisma or accomplishments. It is our presence, prayer and availability for the Holy Spirit to flow through us.

PRESENCE

God simply wants us in the game. He calls for our presence in our neighborhoods, marketplaces, seats of government... wherever people are, He wants us there. He knows we will not be comfortable—we are not supposed to be. He knows we will stand out—that is the idea. He knows we will be hated—that's why He prayed for us. He wants representatives—people to reflect Him—and that's us!

The attack on the World Trade Center, on September 11, 2001, brought the responsibility of first responders clearly into focus for us. These brave men and women knew the danger of the situation, but they ran to it anyway. Their instinct probably told them to run from the danger, but their training told them to run to it. They ignored their flesh and obeyed their calling.

Perilous times have enveloped our world. It is dark and getting darker every day. We want to find a safe place to hide but the call of God is to invade the darkness. His plan is to move through us to bring light, hope and direction to people desperately in need. He intends to use us to be ministers with our presence.

PRAYER

Faster than a speeding bullet, more powerful than a locomotive, able to leap tall buildings in a single bound—that is what they said about Superman. This mythical superhero of my childhood could overcome any challenge thrown at him during a thirty-minute TV show. He was the man!

Well...Superman is not real. He was a made-up character intended for our entertainment. But there is a powerful force accessible to us that can overcome challenges, change situations and accomplish the impossible—that powerful force is prayer.

When righteous people fervently pray, something happens. Reading about prayer does not do it. Talking about prayer does not do it. Serving prayer as an appetizer will not be enough—it must be the entrée. When prayer becomes a priority, the most difficult of situations will change. God is calling and this world needs us to be people of fervent prayer.

AVAILABILITY FOR THE HOLY SPIRIT TO FLOW THROUGH US

A lot of pressure is removed from me when I fully understand, all I am is a vessel through which the Holy Spirit flows. God is not depending on my talent or ability—He has everything and is everything. He just lets me be involved in what He is doing by serving as a portal for the flow of His Spirit.

Again, this is His plan. He could do His work through any method of His choosing—His chosen method is us! He positions us in places where He wants to work. These places may bring pain and be unpleasant, but He is using us. We may not see any value or benefit from our situation, but He is working. We may not understand or even see an outcome in this life, but His plan is being achieved. Our responsibility is simply to be available and obey. His great delight is when we surrender to His will and His work is fulfilled through us. Our testing time becomes a testimony and our obedience becomes an answer to someone's prayer. In all of this process, Jesus is glorified and a difference is made through us.

I am confident we can all agree, our world is in bad shape. We can spend hours talking about what we are seeing and where it appears we are heading—that will not help. We can accept the fate of society and just hope we can hang on long enough to escape—that is a poor plan. We can write our obituary and give up—that is the worst plan of all.

I choose to see God on His throne. I choose to remember the shed blood of Jesus. I choose to stand upon the Word of God. I choose to believe God is still at work in this world and it "ain't over til it's over!"

I may want to run—I'll run to Him. I may want to hide—I'll hide in Him. He will be my strength, my shield, my defense. He will not leave me alone. I will never be forsaken.

Yes, things are looking rough, and we are not in Mayberry any longer, but God still has a plan—that plan involves us. He has brought us into the Kingdom for a time just like this. We have no alternative but to accept it and be who He is calling us to be. It is the right thing to do. The world really does need us.

LEADERSHIP THOUGHTS

AN EXERCISE IN CONTEMPLATION
Placing What I Just Read Into My Ministry Context

1. What are your takeaways from this chapter? How can it be applied to your life and ministry?

2. What are some challenges you face in your service to the Lord? How does it make you feel to know Jesus prayed for you in John 17? What is your response to this prayer?

3. Are you available for God to use however He desires? Have you fully surrendered every area of your life to Him? How are you attempting to be effective in this world? Are you willing for God to stretch you to make an even greater difference?

PRAYER ASSIGNMENT

Spend some time praying for specific needs around you. Ask God to shape and mold you to be a vessel He can use to reach out to these needs. Pray for boldness and confidence in Him. Be open for the Holy Spirit to lead you to people He wants to touch. Thank Him for allowing you to be part of His plan. Believe God for the miraculous!

CHAPTER 27

But The Church Prayed

(Posted June 16, 2023)

The book of Acts reads like an adventure movie meant for the big screen. Beginning with the supernatural birth of the Church and continuing through its amazing growth and impact, each page is alive detailing the action of the Holy Spirit in the lives of everyday, ordinary human beings. The book is filled with heroes and villains, inspiration and drama, as well as information and instruction. It is a powerful account of life directed by the Holy Spirit.

One of my favorite stories in Acts is found in the 12th chapter. It begins with a wicked king bringing persecution to the Church. King Herod killed James and has plans to do the same to Peter. He has Peter arrested and placed in prison. He carefully and strategically placed the apostle in an inner cell surrounded by armed guards and the plan is to execute him after Passover... but the Church prayed.

The night before Peter was set to appear before the king, an angel of the Lord entered the prison cell, miraculously removed Peter's chains, and led him safely outside the prison—without the guards even seeing it! You really need to read this story! It is just one example, in the book of Acts, of God's response to a praying Church.

The obvious point of Acts is the powerful working of the Holy Spirit. But as you carefully dissect the recorded moments of the New Testament Church, an underlying element that must not be missed is, this Church prayed. Prayer was not relegated to an event or a duty, it was a lifestyle. Prayer was not seen as a last resort after everything else was tried, it was the first line of defense and a primary weapon in their arsenal. Prayer was not seen as religious activity; it was what they were called to do...and God answered their prayers.

Throughout history, the people of God have faced great challenges but have overcome because they called on God in prayer and He answered them.

In the Old Testament—

- God's people are surrounded and being attacked by enemy nations...but they prayed, and God delivered them.
- They came under the authority of wicked kings and governments who brought idols and massive perversion to the forefront...but they prayed, and God intervened.
- They faced times of famine and pestilence...but they prayed, and God provided and protected.
- They failed God and turned away from Him...but they prayed and repented, and God restored them.
- They followed God's direction and built a tabernacle in which God would dwell...and as they prayed and offered their sacrifices to Him, fire fell from Heaven and the presence of God went with them.

In the New Testament—

- The Church faced immense persecution...but they prayed, and God delivered them.
- They faced times of great need...but they prayed, and God brought great miracles to them.
- They faced times of controversy and question...but they prayed, and God gave direction.
- They faced times of sickness—even death...but they prayed, and God healed and brought resurrection.
- They hungered for God and His power...and as they prayed God manifested His presence and brought revival—one time even causing the place to shake where they prayed!

In our own lifetime, we have witnessed and experienced perilous times. We have seen political unrest, natural disasters and moral depravity. We have walked through the valley of the shadow of death and had our faith stretched to the nth degree. We have encountered attacks from without and within, yet we are still standing. We are overcomers, not because of our personal strength and ability, but because the Church prayed. Prayer has been the secret sauce (not really a secret) that has sustained us and carried us through every storm.

Today, the Church finds itself in a strange land. Like the people of God in Psalm 137, some have lost hope—hung their harps in the willows—and accepted the fact our best days are behind us. These have stopped singing the Lord's song and have moved into survival mode.

While some in today's Church are simply hanging on, others have allowed themselves (maybe without even realizing it) to become distracted by things that seem important but have little, if any, eternal value. While the world is on a collision course with disaster, these have chosen to spend their time debating worship aesthetics, who gets a seat at the table, and what our titles should be. These arguments are rarely settled and lend more to divide us than to bring us together.

I think it is time to take a deep breath and revisit some history. A trip through the Scriptures and a walk down memory lane will reveal to us that past conflicts and battles have been settled when the Church prayed. Prayer has unveiled strategies for victory and enlisted the army of Heaven to come to our defense. Prayer has changed attitudes and brought unity to the Body when it did not seem possible. Every believer can testify to the fact, prayer has been the common denominator to every divine intervention.

The Church—the Body of Christ, not the institution—is a force in this world. When it shakes off passivity and operates in its God-ordained authority, it has the power to loose and bind. All the combined forces of hell are no match for the Church. This power is our heritage, available because of the presence of the Holy Spirit but activated when the Church prays.

The challenges of this age are intense. We are being bombarded everyday with hellish attacks intended to take us out. It is not going to get better—evil will get worse and worse. But as in times past, the Church will pray—not just study it, preach about it or meditate on it. We will pray in faith. We will pray boldly. We will pray together in agreement. And just as in times past, God will answer by confirming His Word and doing *"exceedingly abundantly above all that we ask or think, according to the power that works in us."* (Ephesians 3:20)

It's not time to stop singing the Lord's song. It's not time to give in to bureaucratic or institutional tendencies. It's certainly not time to operate in fear. It is time to pray. When the Church prays, things change. We have evidence to this fact. But the church prayed…

AN EXERCISE IN CONTEMPLATION
Placing What I Just Read Into My Ministry Context

1. What are your takeaways from this chapter? How can it be applied to your life and ministry?

2. On a scale of 1-10, how important is prayer to you? On average, how much time do you pray each day? Is your prayer life powerful and productive? Are you pleased with your prayer life? Is God pleased with your prayer life?

3. What are some obstacles you face in your prayer life? What can you do to overcome these? Are you intentionally working to develop a more powerful prayer life?

PRAYER ASSIGNMENT

Be intentional to carve out some time in your daily schedule to be alone with God (do not let guilt stop you even if you only have a few minutes). Enter into His presence with praise and thanksgiving. Let your faith arise as you remember the many times He has intervened for you. Boldly bring your petitions and requests knowing He has invited you to do so. Expect Him to hear and answer your prayer.

CHAPTER 28

Even When Your Faith Is Not Strong

(Posted July 18, 2023)

One of the most revealing examples of genuine transparency in the Bible is found in Mark 9. A desperate father brings his son to Jesus in need of a miracle. The son is being tormented by evil spirits and there seems to be no help for him. This father has obviously heard of Jesus and sees the Lord as his only hope. In true humility, he says to the Lord, *"...if you can do anything, have compassion on us and help us."* (Mark 9:22)

Jesus responds to the sincere plea of this gentleman by saying, *"If you can believe, all things are possible to him who believes."* (Mark 9:23) Then in a moment of true honesty and with his humanity on full display, the father, with tears streaming down his face, says, *"...Lord, I believe; help my unbelief!"* (Mark 9:24)

I understand this guy! I think he is saying, "Lord, I know your reputation and record. I have seen and heard what you have done for others. I do not doubt your power, but I am having a tough time believing you are going to do it for me." There is no attempt to be super spiritual or something he is not; he simply admits his struggle to believe for this long-dealt-with situation. He knows Jesus can, but will He?

Most of us, if we are honest, can say we have been where this father is in Mark 9. We would never admit to doubting the power of God, because we do not. We have witnessed, and even experienced, His divine intervention many times. But the storm we are presently going through has been raging for quite a long time and there seems to be no end in sight. We have prayed but no change of any size has happened. We do not want to verbally express it, but we are starting to wonder if this prayer will ever be answered. We believe God is able...but nothing happening right now indicates He is going to.

If it has not happened to you yet—get ready! At some point in your walk with God, your faith will be tested. A bad doctor's report...a fractured relationship...a sudden reversal in your finances—a disappointing decision made by someone you love—these and other negative life situations lead to some very anxious moments where your faith experiences the fire. But, of everything that can happen, nothing causes a believer more stress than to pray—earnestly pray and believe—only for it to seem the walls of Heaven are brass, and you simply cannot break through. You believe, but your circumstances have inserted some unbelief into the equation. What do you do now?

The answer to this important question is actually not as difficult as the enemy of your soul wants you to think it is. The omnipotent, omnipresent, omniscient, and eternal God is also your Heavenly Father, who loves you more than you can comprehend. He cares deeply about your need and is concerned about everything that concerns you. When times of trial come your way, the devil wants to confuse you and make you afraid, but God has a simple strategy to bring you through to a place of peaceful confidence where His will is understood and can be embraced. It is discovered through four simple steps:

TRUST GOD

God is good. He loves us and everything He does is for our good. He has the big picture of our life in mind at all times and His sovereignty is never lost in our situation. Your present reality does not define you. You are, and always will be, who and what God says. Our beautiful and wonderful God can always be trusted!

LISTEN TO GOD

God has a good plan for your life. This plan can only be received through intimacy with the Father. During these sacred moments of communion with Him, He teaches and shapes us. The lessons He wants us to learn during these times are revelatory and life changing. His Word and will come alive as we listen intently for His Spirit.

KEEP LOOKING TO GOD

Do not give up! God is not restricted to your facts or the expert's opinion. Regardless of your present landscape, do not stop praying...press through your unbelief...keep your head up—even through tears and fears. God does His best work when things seem impossible. His answer to your prayer will come.

TRUST GOD (YES, I SAID IT AGAIN!)

The journey to breakthrough is enveloped in trusting God. True peace and contentment only come when the warring ends and the trusting begins. This does not mean you accept your present situation, but it does mean you accept the Father's perfect will for your life. This can be done when you become convinced His plan for you is nothing short of amazing. I say it again—our beautiful and wonderful God can be trusted.

The story I have referenced from Mark 9 is so encouraging because we see the only response Jesus gave to the visible humanity of a broken father was to heal the man's son. There was no rebuke for the unbelief and no theological discourse on the importance of faith—Jesus just met the need and brought an end to the life-long struggle for this family. Even when faith was weak, His power and compassion were at work.

This lesson was made clear to the disciples of Jesus one night while they were sailing on the Sea of Galilee. The story in Mark 4 tells us, as they made their way across the sea this particular evening, a great storm arose. This storm was so intense, the disciples feared for their lives. They did all they knew to do to keep the ship together and heading in the right direction, but it looked like, in spite of their best efforts, they were going down in that storm. Finally, someone remembered Jesus was on board—asleep in the back of the boat—but was not helping them. In desperation, they cried out "Lord, get up and help us! We are about to die! Don't you care?"

The Scripture says Jesus got up, calmly surveyed the situation, and said to the sea, "Peace, be still." The storm immediately stopped and there was perfect calm.

The disciples in this story did not respond to this horrific storm in faith—they were scared to death! This lack of faith did not keep Jesus from intervening—He got up at their cry and rebuked the wind and waves. Jesus did this, not because of their great faith but, because they (the disciples) were His! His love for them brought His miraculous intervention.

The two stories from the Bible in this article have a common denominator—real people faced real situations with weak faith at best. Of course God would have been more pleased if great faith had been in operation, but the realities of the situation did not stop the love of God from being demonstrated. This reality was simple—God knew the hearts of these men and they belonged to Him! He moved for them—not because of their faith but because of His love.

You, too, are dearly loved by the Lord. He knows you—all of your issues, all of your disappointments, all of your fears. He calls you His own and the reason for your creation has not changed. He wants to give you fulfillment in a life of God-awareness and blessing. He will never fail to keep His Word to you—you can count on it.

Without sounding harsh, the choice is actually yours. You can seclude yourself in a world of unfulfilled dreams, or you can wrap yourself up in the love of a Father who will never let you down. He is waiting for your decision. You can cry out to Him anytime and He will hear you and help you...even when your faith is not strong.

AN EXERCISE IN CONTEMPLATION
Placing What I Just Read Into My Ministry Context

1. What are your takeaways from this chapter? How can it be applied to your life and ministry?

2. How willing are you to continue praying and believing for long-dealt-with situations in your life? Do you, sometimes, feel this prayer will never be answered? How does the story in Mark 9 speak to you in this situation?

3. What lessons have you learned while waiting on God to answer your prayer? How can these lessons be used to help others struggling with similar issues in their life? Are you willing for God to use you help others?

PRAYER ASSIGNMENT

Do not be afraid to admit your humanity to God when you pray. Confess your fear, doubt, and confusion to Him as you lay your need before His throne. Remind yourself of His greatness and let Him know you are His no matter what. Listen intently for His peaceful voice and look for rest in Him. As you praise Him, expect peace that passes understanding.

CHAPTER 29

Sometimes Praying Is Not Enough

(Posted August 26, 2023)

I was blessed to grow up in a small classical Pentecostal church. I have so many impressionable memories from this time in my life. The people and experiences in this little church, no doubt, make me the man I am today. I am very thankful for my heritage!

One of the things a guest to our church would quickly notice was our language. We had phrases we understood but probably no one else did. We would say things like, "you need to grab hold of the horns of the altar and stay there until you pray through." Well...our altar didn't have horns. It was a long piece of wood with molded edges that had been varnished and lacquered. It was actually quite beautiful, but it had no horns. We knew we were being instructed to kneel at the altar and stay there until we got the victory, but I am certain an outsider had no clue.

When we knelt at the altar we were never there alone. People in the church always gathered around and prayed with whomever was kneeling there. I still remember the language of the altar. Someone on my right side would tell me to "let go" while someone on my left side was telling me to "hang on." This was not confusing to me because I knew the language. Both of my prayer partners were on the same page. They were encouraging me to be determined in my prayer and not let anything hinder me. I can only imagine the confusion, however, for someone new to that experience.

There was another phrase that would come up from time to time that, I am sure, made no sense to anyone who did not speak our language. In the pastor's sermon or in someone's testimony they would say, "sometimes you have to put legs to your prayer." I am sure this one caused any newcomer to our church to wonder if we offered a PSL class (Pentecost as a Second

Language)! We knew we were being reminded, there are times you have to work along with your prayer, but the images this phrase produced in the mind of those who did not understand had to make for some interesting conversations with their non-Pentecostal friends!

My mind pulled up the "putting legs to your prayer" idea recently while reading about the Children of Israel crossing the Red Sea. Moses has led his people out of Egypt, and they are on their way to the land God promised them many years earlier. They came to the mighty Red Sea, however, and it looks like their emancipation will end in their destruction. There is no way to cross this large body of water, and Pharaoh and his army have had a change of heart about allowing the Israelites to leave—they are now in hot pursuit of their former slaves.

The Children of Israel get scared and, in their fear, they begin to complain. They see no solution to their dilemma and feel certain their annihilation is imminent. In this desperate situation, God gives another strong word to Moses, and he shares it with the people:

"Do not be afraid. Stand still, and see the salvation of the Lord, which He will accomplish for you today. For the Egyptians whom you see today, you shall see again no more forever. The Lord will fight for you, and you shall hold your peace." (Exodus 14:13-14)

Evidently, this word was not enough for Moses and his people because the next verse takes a more stern tone, as God says to them, *"Why do you cry to Me? Tell the children of Israel to go forward."* (Exodus 14:15) He seems to be saying, "It is time to stop praying and start moving." I think He is saying to them it is time to put legs to their prayers!

I am certain God wants me to be a man of prayer. I believe my private prayer life will largely determine the effectiveness of my public ministry. Prayer should always be a primary weapon in my arsenal and my prayer life should be so powerful it causes

SOMETIMES PRAYING IS NOT ENOUGH

the devil to tremble in fear. But with all that being said, there comes a time when praying is not enough.

Most of the promises of the Lord have conditions attached. He makes a contract with us, telling us what He expects from us and what we will receive from Him if we do our part. This contract—or covenant—is etched in stone and will not be compromised. We do our part; He does His.

I've discovered, many times our blessing is not realized because we are continually praying for God to do what He has promised, while all the time He is waiting for us to meet His set condition. Prayer and fasting, the laying on of hands, counseling—you name it—nothing is going to move the hand of God until we live up to the contract. We must put legs to our prayer.

This principle is beautifully illustrated by the story of Naaman in II Kings 5. Naaman is a national hero among the Syrian people, but he has been stricken with the dreaded disease of leprosy. He hears about a prophet named Elisha whom, he is told, heals people with this sickness. Naaman makes his way to the prophet's house and, as he pulls into the drive, Naaman sends one of his servants to the door to request the attention of Elisha. Elisha hears the problem, but instead of coming out to personally address Naaman, he sends out instruction for Naaman to go wash seven times in the Jordan River.

This is certainly not the reception and treatment Naaman was expecting. As a matter of fact, he is highly offended at the lack of personal attention he received from Elisha, and even more offended he was told he had to wash in the muddy Jordan River. He is so put off by this, he leaves the prophet's residence in a rage. He left in anger, with his pride intact...and with his leprosy.

After a little cooling off period, one of Naaman's servants attempted to reason with him. He encouraged his master to simply do what the prophet had instructed. Naaman knows it is the right thing to do, so he submits. He heads for the Jordan ready to swallow his pride and obey.

In my mind, I see Naaman stepping out of his chariot in humiliation and embarrassment. He would rather be a million other places than on the banks of the Jordan River, but this is what the prophet said he had to do to be healed of this disease. It wouldn't surprise me if he was thinking, "Maybe my willingness to come here will be enough for the God of Elisha to heal me." But it wasn't.

He steps into the water and dips one time. He may have looked at his skin to see if God would show mercy and heal him because of his humble submission to the prophet's instruction. But God didn't.

He dipped 2...3...4...5...6 times and there is no change whatsoever. He quickly submerged himself one more time in the river and—you guessed it—he came out of the water completely healed. The Scripture says, *"...His flesh was restored like the flesh of a little child, and he was clean."* (II Kings 5:14) Naaman had fulfilled his part of the contract; God did not fail to fulfill his part as well.

So many times God speaks to us and gives us an assignment. This assignment is His plan for our life and there is a beautiful blessing promised as we obey. This is God's covenant with us— we follow His direction, and He gives the blessing. There is no negotiation involved, no deal making, no gamesmanship, just total surrender and obedience. We obey; God honors His word.

Unfortunately, too often our attention is on the blessing. We continually pray for God to give us what we desire—what we need. We call others to pray for us and feel, because of our strong petition, God will relent and give what we are asking. But here is God's word for us today, no amount of praying is going to bring the answer we are seeking. It is not a matter of praying; it is a matter of obedience. God has already made a promise; the promise will be kept when the contract is fulfilled.

There are some blessings that will never come to you, no matter how much you pray. Sometimes praying is not enough. The blessing that seems just out of your grasp may well be waiting on your total submission to the will of God for your life. This should not be seen as trying to earn your answered prayer; it should be seen as keeping your side of the contract. God will do His part, no doubt. You might just need to put legs to your prayer.

LEADERSHIP THOUGHTS

AN EXERCISE IN CONTEMPLATION
Placing What I Just Read Into My Ministry Context

1. What are your takeaways from this chapter? How can it be applied to your life and ministry?

2. What has God called you to do? Are you fully submitting to this call?

3. What do you feel is a reason for unanswered prayer in your life? Could there be a need to put legs to your prayers? What action do you feel God is expecting from you in order for you to fulfill your side of the covenant?

PRAYER ASSIGNMENT

Use this time to renew your commitment to the Lord. Intentionally move beyond the knowledge of Jesus as your Savior and fully embrace Him as Lord of your life. Seek Him for His will and affirm your desire to fully align with it. As He speaks to you, be ready to obey. Praise Him for the life-changing victory heading your way!

CHAPTER 30

He Sees, He Knows And Payday Is Coming

(Posted October 13, 2023)

I grew up in southeast Oklahoma in the heart of tornado alley. I have many vivid memories, as a little boy, joining other members of my extended family in my grandmother's underground cellar, while we waited for storms to pass. This was a common occurrence in the springtime in our little part of the world. The sights, sounds and even smells of these times will forever be embedded in my mind.

Weather forecasting was not as sophisticated then as it is now. It seemed most afternoons and evenings in the spring were the same—we would be under a tornado watch. We were taught a tornado watch meant conditions were right for a tornado—this was so common it did not produce much concern. Things would heat up, however, when we were under a tornado warning. The warning meant a tornado had actually been spotted. The Oakes siblings and their children (my mother's family) did not have to be told twice what to do when a tornado warning was issued—we headed for the cellar!

Meteorology has advanced greatly from those days I have referenced here. Radars have become so highly developed and complex. Today, a tornado warning will be issued before a funnel is ever visibly seen because radar is capable of seeing them before people can. These radars are so accurate, they will tell you what time your community—even your street address— can expect the storm to pass over. It is amazing! If these had existed in my childhood I probably wouldn't have this nervous twitch every time I think of that damp musty storm cellar in my grandmother's back yard!

The state-of-the-art, ultramodern tools available to forecast weather, today, have nothing on the heavenly radar God has been using since the beginning of time (I know God does not need or use radar, but work with me here!). Nothing has ever gotten by the Father. Solomon wrote, *"The eyes of the Lord are in every place, Keeping watch on the evil and the good."* (Proverbs 15:3) He sees our behavior, discerns our motives, and knows the very dictates of our hearts. He does not miss a thing.

From childhood, I was taught this fact—God is always watching. This lesson was usually given in the context of improper behavior. From songs we sang to Sunday School lessons—from fiery Sunday night sermons to parental discipline—I knew I could not get away with anything. I have to admit, even to this day, if I forget to take my gum out of my mouth when I enter the sanctuary or forget to say the blessing over my meal, I quickly repent for fear I may miss the rapture if it occurred right then! I did not hear a whole lot about grace as a child, but the "living right" part was made crystal clear! Obviously, there is some exaggeration here, but those of you raised as I was know this is not too far from how it really was!

Lately I have been giving a great deal of thought to the flip side to this coin—God doesn't just see the bad things going on in the world, but He is also taking note of the faithfulness of His people. Every day, committed Christians are serving and looking for ways to please the Lord—not for praise or fame but just because it is what they do. Doing the will of God is simply in the DNA of a disciple of Jesus and no good deed will go unnoticed or unrewarded by our heavenly Father.

Throughout my life I have been influenced by men and women who, without recognition or notoriety, have faithfully served the Lord. They have been small church pastors, missionaries in remote parts of the world, laity who sacrificed to support ministry, people who loved God more than anything and were willing to give all to serve Him. These folks will never have their stories written in a book or receive great accolades in this world. The spotlight will never be on them and few people outside their circle will ever hear about them, but God has seen—He knows—and payday is coming!

I am grateful for Godly leaders who have a platform and use it carefully to proclaim the full Gospel of the Lord, Jesus. There are many humble men and women, whom God has called to prominent places, and their voices are a clarion call in this sinful age. But as I consider the big picture of the Kingdom, I am convinced the greatest impact is being made by the unseen warriors who pray in the closet, give in secret, and daily take up their cross and follow Him. These are the movers and shakers. These are those who strike fear in the devil himself. These are the ones who have been faithful over a few things but will be made ruler over many.

A winning football team is usually known for its star quarterback or running back. Occasionally there will be a defensive player who gets a lot of press time but, rarely, will the offensive linemen get the attention they deserve. These big guys who line up in the trenches, nose to nose against the opposing team, may not get the mentions some other players get, but their success will always determine the success of the team. If they do their job well, the chances of their team winning increase greatly. If they fail to do their job, the chance for victory is tremendously decreased.

These offensive linemen may not get the public attention they deserve but I guarantee, their coach notices. When the film from the previous game is being reviewed, that coach will always see the fulfilled assignments of his players. Great satisfaction comes to the player and the coach when they know the job was well done. The fulfillment of the assignment is enough to motivate the selfless player to suit up for another game next week.

We are in the game of our life—it is a game of life or death. The regular season has concluded and the playoffs are in full swing. The season is almost over. I cannot stop—I cannot even slow down. I cannot be concerned with what position I am called to play. I cannot be moved by the cheers from the crowd or the lack thereof. I have a job to do. I must get it done. I will be rewarded, not for my talent or skill, but for my faithfulness. I want to be faithful whatever the cost.

I sometimes wonder, if the Apostle Paul were to come to our church, today, and preach one sermon, what would he preach? There is so much he wrote that would be appropriate for us, but it would not surprise me if he took his text from I Corinthians 15:58—

"Therefore, my beloved brethren, be steadfast, immovable, always abounding in the work of the Lord, knowing that your labor is not in vain in the Lord."

This is the message for every believer. Keep standing. Be determined. Keep serving. Be faithful. God is watching and He is keeping good records. He sees when no one else does and He has a magnificent reward, that will never fade away, awaiting those who finish well. That is the goal for which we are striving—to finish strong and hear Him say, "Well done." That will be our final victory. It is coming soon!

AN EXERCISE IN CONTEMPLATION
Placing What I Just Read Into My Ministry Context

1. What are your takeaways from this chapter? How can it be applied to your life and ministry?

2. Who are those in your life who have influenced you most to serve God? What have they done to make such a profound impact on your life? How are you impacting others?

3. When God sees your service and commitment, is He pleased? Are there areas in your spiritual walk that need improvement? If so, what are these areas? What are you doing to make the needed improvement?

> **PRAYER ASSIGNMENT**
>
> Spend some time thanking God for His marvelous grace extended to you. Thank Him for the Godly examples He has brought into your life and the impact they have made. Commit to the Father your desire to not just be a taker, but to be a real giver. Pray specifically for opportunities to serve Him by serving others. Determine in your prayer to finish well and hear Him say to you, "Well done!"

CHAPTER 31

Do Not—And I Repeat—Do Not Drink The Poison

(Posted January 30, 2024)

DO NOT—AND I REPEAT—DO NOT DRINK THE POISON

It is called the silent killer. It has no odor, no color and emits no fumes. Several hundred people die from it each year and, because of it, many more suffer debilitating illnesses. I am talking about carbon monoxide poisoning. It can strike anytime, anywhere and, unless there is a detector present, you do not see it coming.

It is a terrible thing to encounter a deadly poison like this, but it is even worse to have it present with you and not know it. You are just living your life, but at the same time breathing toxic air that could kill you. You are in the presence of death, but you are unaware.

This is a very dark and morbid illustration to begin my blog, and very different from the pattern I usually follow but, today, my spirit is stirred. I believe there is so much God wants to do among His people, and I want to see and be part of it. But the more I pray and the closer I look, I keep seeing forces at work to hinder the breakthrough God wants to give. These barriers have existed for so long they are no longer recognized as problems by many. They have become ingrained into our fabric and accepted as normal. Truth is, they are a trojan horse that has been allowed to come into our camp with an intent to stymie and, eventually, destroy us.

We are sometimes reluctant to take a critical look inward. It is very uncomfortable to admit the greatest problem in our lives, and in our churches, does not lie outside but looks back at us in the mirror every morning. It is only when the realization of this fact strikes a chord in our heart that we will address it with sincere repentance and a strong willingness to change. Now is the time for this realization to be made.

I do not pretend to know all or have all the answers, but as I pray, three big problems keep coming to my mind as tools the enemy is using to hold us back and keep us from being as effective as we need to be in this troubled world. These are not problems around us, but in us. They do not exist everywhere, but they are prevalent enough to be concerning. Here is what I hear the Lord saying to me.

FAILURE TO BE THE CHURCH

We focus on having church and have strong opinions as to what that means. We give much attention to logistics and mechanics that make us relevant to the present culture. We fail to realize these things do not matter nearly as much to God as they do to us. His desire for us is that we BE the Church He purchased with His own blood.

We are not this Church through our denominational connection. We are not this Church because we used to be this Church. We are not this Church because of our published doctrinal positions. We are this Church when we do three things: preach the Word, live the Word and experience the Word.

We are told in Scripture the end times will be marked by preaching that lacks truth and is meant to please people. There is no doubt we are there. In too many places, preaching is no longer seen as important, and its watered-down content is no longer productive. The true Church must make the decision to swim upstream by boldly and lovingly preaching the full Gospel. We can leave nothing out. We must reprove, rebuke and exhort with long-suffering and doctrine. I believe we will be judged as much for what we *do not* say as we are for what we *do* say. We must preach the Word.

Preaching the Word must transition into living the Word. The practical application of the Word into our everyday lives will impact the world and bring souls into the Kingdom. This must be more than a feel-good campaign at Christmas or a monetary contribution to a ministry. We must accept that our mission as the Church is to be the hands and feet of Jesus in a world that desperately needs evidence, God is real. Sunday morning worship is important, but in the Kingdom, so is a cup of coffee with an unsaved friend, a warm coat for the homeless man under the bridge, and a kind word to the stressed mother in the check-out line. Opportunities to live the Word are endless…we must stay prepared to see and do.

When the Word of God is preached with conviction and the people of God take seriously their mission in the world, the Holy Spirit is ready to reveal Himself in powerful ways by bringing the experiences of the New Testament Church into our reality. We cease to be a weak, anemic body, whose past is brighter than its future, and we become a Church alive in the power of the Spirit. Miracles, signs and wonders stop being talking points and begin to happen. Answered prayer is no longer a surprise and expectancy replaces uncertainty. This is God's plan for His Church.

For so long there has been a wide chasm between what we preach and what we experience. Many have slipped into a "form of godliness with no power" existence—we know how to have church, but we are weak when it comes to being the church. It is time for this to end. We must, again, become a force in this world by being the Church all the power of hell cannot prevail against.

CARNALITY WITHIN THE CHURCH

Many local churches, as well as denominations, have been weakened by carnality within the ranks of leadership. In most cases, I am sure, it is unintentional, but it is happening, nonetheless. This attempt to do the work of the Spirit in the flesh has brought the church more in line with the world than with the Word.

In the world, alliances are created to elevate men and agendas. People are used for selfish gain. Voices of the mighty drown out the voices of the weak. Who you are, who you know and where you are from are the determining factors for promotion. What seems right by a powerful few becomes the law of the land.

Sadly, these things are becoming more and more prevalent, not only in the world, but in the church. They have crept in under the guise of protecting and moving the church forward. The back room has replaced the prayer closet, and the politician has replaced the prophet. The goal has become the majority vote, and the voice of the Spirit has been silenced by the will of the people. Instead of the church standing out, it is blending in. This carnal, fleshly approach to ministry and church business is producing discouragement among those who see it, division among those involved in it, and grave danger to those affected by it. God cannot be pleased.

The Church is *in* the world but not *of* the world. We will face the temptation to operate according to what seems right to us, but this carnal approach to leadership must be avoided at all costs. Flesh cannot take the Church where God wants it to go, and the unsanctified will of man will always be an adversary of the Spirit. The prayer of our Lord just before His crucifixion must be ours as well—*"...Not my will, but yours be done."* (Luke 22:42) The sacrificing of our will and our submission to His is the only way to defeat the enemy of carnality.

SELF-PRESERVATION

A telltale sign an organization has become an institution is when the vast amount of our time, energy and resources are used simply to maintain said organization. Mission and vision become secondary to personal agendas and self-promotion. Purpose becomes diluted by gratuitous and self-serving decisions. An institution is all about self-preservation.

Churches and other religious organizations battle this spirit every day. The passion and fire that birthed us give way to survival mode. We hesitate to launch out into uncharted waters because we are "playing not to lose." Our fear of losing is greater than our confidence of winning. We just want to be standing at the end of the day—however that looks.

The church of today cannot fall prey to this mindset. We must catch a fresh vision of who we are and why we are here. We are the Body of Christ. We belong to Him. We represent Him. He bought us with His blood, filled us with His Spirit and called us into His service. We have a job to do, all the while knowing our chief responsibility is to obey Him. Nothing we are called to do is about us, it is all about Him. Our role is not as important as His and our commitment is to follow His lead not our ambition. We must decrease that He may increase.

One of the saddest stories in the Bible is that of Samson in the book of Judges. This mighty man, who had been used greatly by God, reached a point where he took his anointing for granted and placed himself in a compromising position with a woman whose goal was to destroy him. That fateful night, as he slept in the lap of Delilah, his power was taken from him and Judges 16:20 says, *"...He did not know that the Lord had departed from him."* He did not know...he did not know...he did not know the Lord had departed from him.

There is poison running through the church, and like Samson, many are not aware. Its intent is to render us powerless and, eventually, destroy us. In some places it is disguised, and other places it is accepted as no big deal. But be sure, whatever the opinion and whatever the response, poison makes one sick and, sometimes, it kills. It must be detected, and it must be eliminated. We simply cannot tolerate its existence.

Not everyone is deceived by the poison. There is a remnant that is standing strong and determined to remain faithful. This remnant will not be distracted and will not be overcome. They will remain attached to the Word, committed to the Lordship of Jesus and determined to complete the tasks for which they have been commissioned. They understand, they are their brother's keeper and future generations are depending on them. Nothing is more important than their assignment. They are determined to finish strong.

These are critical times. Gamesmanship and manipulation in the Body of Christ must stop. Spiritual leadership must rise to the top and His Kingdom must replace ours. We do not have much time left and there is still much to do. Our goal must be to *"...lay aside every weight, and the sin which so easily ensnares us, and let us run with patience the race that is set before us."* (Hebrews 12:1)

And by all means, do not drink the poison.

AN EXERCISE IN CONTEMPLATION
Placing What I Just Read Into My Ministry Context

1. What are your takeaways from this chapter? How can it be applied to your life and ministry?

2. Does your life and ministry align fully with God's Word? As you consider this question, are there areas where you sense the Holy Spirit's conviction? What is your response to this convicting from the Holy Spirit in your life and ministry?

3. Are you willing to be part of the remnant that will fully follow the Lord in this day and hour? What must you do to ensure you are, indeed, part of this remnant?

PRAYER ASSIGNMENT

Begin your prayer by requesting conviction where conviction is needed and be willing to repent where repentance is needed. Let this be an opportunity to realign with God's will and receive a fresh touch from the Holy Spirit to move forward. Determine to lay aside all things that hold you back. Praise Him for the work He is doing in your life and ministry and recommit to being a vessel He can use in these important days.

CHAPTER 32

Some Things For You To Think About

(Social Media Posts)

- ✓ Challenge of the times—being able to make changes while holding the line for things that must not change. We must learn the difference between systemic change and Kingdom absolutes.

- ✓ Never ask God to take you somewhere you have never been unless you are willing to do something you have never done. Anything of value will always have a price attached.

- ✓ Do not be shocked when business as usual generates only the usual business.

- ✓ Every situation you experience has a lesson to learn. My advice—learn it so you do not have to repeat that class!

- ✓ Genuine freedom comes when you are able to let go and let God. Looking anywhere else leads to bondage. God's will is for you to be joyously free!

- ✓ There is never a wasted hurt when you know the Lord. He takes the most difficult seasons and uses them for our good. He is such a good Father!

- ✓ Everything has a price—there is a cost to change and a cost to remain the same. For which are you most willing to pay?

- ✓ I would like to understand but I do not. I would like for things to change but they may not. I would like to be in control, but I am not. BUT...I am safely living in the palm of His hand; I am blessed beyond measure; and I know when it is over I win! I will take it!

- ✓ You have not been forsaken; you are being preserved. God has not forgotten you; His plan for you is still intact. Do not be weary while doing good. Your time for harvest is near.

- ✓ Being able to celebrate those experiencing God's favor is one of the surest ways to find it for yourself.

LEADERSHIP THOUGHTS

- ✓ God is faithful to His Word and keeps His promises. He is not obligated to our calendars or clocks. He operates on His own schedule but is never late—just ask Lazarus!

- ✓ This year I am praying for assignments not appointments; anointing not applause; less of me and more of Him.

- ✓ The Gospel is essential! It is the power of God unto salvation. Now, as never before, it must be released in the world with full force.

- ✓ Do not expect God to open new doors until you have completed your present assignment. Open doors are rewards for obedience not escape from unpleasant tasks.

- ✓ Struggling and quitting are two different things. The struggle is part of the process. Quitting is always the wrong answer.

- ✓ Someone's world could change today with just a little encouragement from you. How about being a world changer? I'm in!

- ✓ God is good with details. If it concerns you, it concerns Him.

- ✓ Even when you think God is silent you can still hear Him. His Word never stops speaking.

- ✓ God does His best work in my life between the prayer and the answer.

- ✓ In this present climate, the key to a church thriving will be a committed team surrounding the Pastor. Never has "every member fitly joined together" been more important.

- ✓ The Church is called to proclaim truth and walk in it. Lord, help me fulfill my call today.

- ✓ The decision to receive Jesus as my Savior was made by faith. I will use that same faith to get me through these troubled times. It works!

- ✓ Success is never determined by a title. Real success is found in the perfect will of God.

- ✓ Refuse to be intimidated or influenced by the expectations of others. Embrace who God has called you to be. Regardless of what anyone says, it is the right thing to do.

- ✓ I do not understand but I trust God. I am uncomfortable but content. I am in the battle of my life, but I am filled with peace. All of this is made possible because of Jesus! Blessed!

- ✓ Be encouraged. The God who spoke the world into existence is at work in your life today!

- ✓ Now is the time for the world to see we believe what we preach...and that it's true!

- ✓ As I pray, today, for our church, I'm asking God to make us lighthouses in our communities; keep us faithful to our mission; and provide all that is needed for us to do what we are called to do. I believe He will do it!

- ✓ Even when you are told to not be afraid, sometimes you still are. Pray anyway. God hears you, not because of your great faith, but because you are His. He is with you. He will not leave you.

- ✓ Trust God to open doors; trust Him to close doors. Trust God to make a way; trust Him to block the way. At all times He is God; in all things He knows best. Trust God.

- ✓ When you cannot see where you are headed, remember where you have been. He did not bring you this far to leave you. I am holding onto this.

- ✓ I want to be successful but not as much as I want to be spiritual. I want to be relevant but not as much as I want to be holy. I do not want to be conformed to the world but transformed by a renewed mind. I believe it is time for me (and the Church) to be different.

- ✓ If it matters to you it matters to God. Go ahead and tell Him where it hurts. He cares.

- ✓ God's great plan for your life will not be found in your breakthrough. Revelation comes while you are waiting. Learn to value the process.

- ✓ Sometimes life is pretty foggy. Your vision is blurred—you cannot see very far in front of you. The best move to make in these times is simply to hold on. Fog always lifts.

- ✓ When every road you take hits a dead end...when the numbness makes it even hard to pray...when nothing you are going through makes sense...stay faithful. That is all He requires.

- ✓ Be thankful and whine not. (Higgins 1:1)

- ✓ Every test and trial have a testimony attached—look for it. We must not fail to tell it.

- ✓ You see an acorn; God sees an oak tree. You were created for more. Believe.

- ✓ In leadership—and in life—flexibility means parameters can be adjusted but sanity requires parameters exist.

- ✓ Do not give up! Keep showing up!

- ✓ An important tool leaders must develop is the ability to filter. Do not be moved by everything you hear, see, or feel. Always consider the source.

- ✓ Life is God's idea! He brought it into existence. His will is that yours be great!

- ✓ In ministry, titles are used to designate responsibilities not determine availability for God to use. He works through whosoever He wills. All are eligible.

- ✓ One cannot be in God's will without being in God's Word.

- ✓ Holding on to my past when God is moving me forward is idolatry. While I appreciate where I have been, I know it was preparing me for where I am going. God's plans are always greater.

- ✓ Four leadership essentials—anointing, wisdom, courage, and favor. Every challenge is overcome with these.

- ✓ There are no shortcuts to spiritual breakthrough. It will only come after total obedience—not before and not until.

- ✓ I do not just want a prayer life; I want to pray big! Never be guilty of praying too small.

- ✓ As a leader, I must constantly ask myself, "Are my actions being directed by the Spirit or driven by my ego?" I must remember God is not obligated to bless plans He has not ordained.

- ✓ Looking at the ministry of Jesus, I discover miracles always followed obedience. This is revelation I do not want to forget.

- ✓ The wilderness is a transitional time where we either look back and elevate the past or look forward and claim the promise. It is our choice.

- ✓ Vision comes from an encounter with God. It is personal and not understood by everyone. It is important for vision to be strong before sharing with others. An early reveal will be misunderstood and take longer to develop.

LEADERSHIP THOUGHTS

- ✓ As a minister of the Gospel who has tasted and seen, I cannot be satisfied to lead people to an experience that feels good but stops with the music. I want to make disciples.

- ✓ Abraham's mountain of great trial became a place of miraculous provision. This will be our testimony, as well, as we submit to the leadership of the Holy Spirit.

- ✓ If I trust God to open doors, I must trust Him to close doors. The same God does both and it is always right and good.

- ✓ Pastor, your family will inevitably make sacrifices in ministry, but your family must not become the sacrifice. Guard your home.

- ✓ The key to ministry victory is knowing the difference between waiting and stalling. We wait for direction from the Lord, but we must be ready to move when He speaks.

- ✓ Commitment to the work of the Lord leads to utter frustration. Commitment to the Lordship of Jesus leads to absolute fulfillment.

- ✓ I want the product; God works through the process. It is what happens between the asking and receiving that makes the greatest difference in my life and ministry.

- ✓ The Church should not expect politicians to do what God has called us to do. Our nation will not be changed at the ballot box but in the prayer closet. "If my people…"

- ✓ I cannot truly make a difference if I am not truly different. Do not let the world squeeze you into its mold.

- ✓ The goal of God's mercy is transformation.

- ✓ The longer I serve in leadership, the more I learn quick decisions are rarely good ones. Gather facts. Pray it through.

- ✓ Red, yellow, black, or white—all are precious in His sight. Racism has no place in the Body. It is called sin.

- ✓ Life is filled with ups and downs but that is not an excuse to be in and out. The call of God is to be steadfast, immovable, always abounding.

- ✓ Church leader, be careful lest your quest for relevance becomes rebellion. Approach God with awe and handle His Word with reverence.

- ✓ A shift in circumstances may require a shift in my attitude and approach. I do not want to admit it, but sometimes I am the problem.

- ✓ Condemnation and conviction are not the same. As a believer I am free from condemnation, but I must never be hardened to conviction.

- ✓ Praying to get is burdensome. Praying to be is liberating.

- ✓ Beware of what you allow in your life. Constantly marching around the same wall ceases to be a battle and becomes a habit.

- ✓ The times do not always call for change; sometimes being steadfast is the answer.

- ✓ Leader, never make things harder than they have to be. Also, do not look for the easy way. Do what is right. Right is always best.

- ✓ Anointing is not for our performance but for His will. God's favor is not for our success but for His glory.

- ✓ The fact I am a child of God is His idea. He really wants to be my Father.

LEADERSHIP THOUGHTS

AN EXERCISE IN CONTEMPLATION
Placing What I Just Read Into My Ministry Context

1. Which quote(s) in this chapter spoke most to you? Why do you think this is the case?

2. Which chapter(s) in this book spoke most to you? Why do you think this is the case?

3. What action(s) do you need to take to become a better leader? How important is it to you to become a better leader? With the knowledge you have gained and the stirring of your spirit, what will your next step(s) be?

PRAYER ASSIGNMENT

Thank God for His call upon your life. Thank Him for the opportunity you have to be involved in ministry and influence lives around you. Confess to Him, as thankful as you are for what He had done for you, you are not satisfied and want to go deeper. Seek a more willing spirit to submit to His plan and a greater anointing to accomplish everything He has for you to do. Let Him know you are ready to go where you have never gone and do what you have never done. Open your heart to hear and receive His direction. Be ready to say yes to whatever He calls you to do. Believe with everything within you, this is your greatest day and nothing can stop what God has started in your life and ministry.

www.ingramcontent.com/pod-product-compliance
Lightning Source LLC
LaVergne TN
LVHW021810060526
838201LV00058B/3310